FIND YOUR WORK

Unlocking Your Path to Impact, Fulfilment, and Worthy Compensation

TOYIN OBAFEMI

Copyright 2024 by Toyin Obafemi

Published by Pnuxel Consulting
toyin@pnuxelconsulting.com

All rights reserved. No part of this book may be reproduced or transmitted in any form or by any means- electronic or mechanical, including photocopying, recording, or by any information storage and retrieval system without the author's written permission except for the inclusion of brief quotations in a review.

CONTENTS

Acknowledgements 6

Introduction 8

Chapter One: Work Is A Blessing And Not A Curse 12

    The Origin of Work 13

    Man Was Created Because There Was Work For Him To Do 15

Chapter Two: Your Job Versus Your Work 25

    Don't Confuse Your Job With Your Work. 26

    More Than What To Do 33

    Think Beyond Your Job 35

    Your Job Is Temporary While Your Work Is Permanent. 40

    Do Not Be Quick To Forget That You Are A Steward. 50

    While On Your Job. 60

    Turn Your Job Into An Opportunity Where You Are Paid To Learn. 72

    Your Job Is Your Career, While Your Work Is Your Life Assignment. 73

    You Can Retire From Your Job But Not Your Work. 74

You Can Be Fired From Your Job But Not Your Work. 77

Your Gift Makes Room For Him 79

Chapter Three: Excel Both In Your Job And Your Life's Work 81
Before You Quit Your Job..82

Secret To Excelling Both In Your Job And Your Life's Work 92

Chapter Four: Simple Steps To Identifying Your Work 98
Discover The 3 Most Important Goals In Your Life: A Quick And Easy Guide 100

Chapter Five: Exploring The Two Dimensions Of Work 104
Engaging Your Creative Ability 106

Is Handwork Without Significance?.......................114

Create Time For Mental Work 116

Israel Demonstrating The Two Dimensions Of Work 117

Chapter Six: Rest Comes After Work. 123
Reaping What You Have Sown: The Law Of Harvest. 123

Do Your Work While You Are Young....................126

Don't Confuse Being Busy With Work. 130

Find Your Work And Engage In It 134

Unlock Your Potential: Discover the Transformative Power of My Other Books 135

The Author 139

References 142

ACKNOWLEDGEMENTS

First and foremost, I want to give all glory and honour to God, the giver of time, life, and opportunity. Without Him, none of this would be possible.

My deepest gratitude goes to my beautiful wife, Temitope, for her unwavering support and encouragement throughout this journey. Her belief in me and this project has been a constant source of motivation. Her love and patience have been invaluable.

I would also like to thank our precious children, Oreofe and Inioluwa, for being a source of inspiration. Their joy and curiosity remind me of the importance of living in the present and making the most of every moment.

I am also deeply grateful to Adewobi Adebanjo for going out of his way to design the cover for this book. You have always been reliable. Thank you!

INTRODUCTION

Some years ago, I found myself in a desperate situation. I had my wife and our newborn son to provide for, bills piling up, and no steady income in sight. I sent out job applications after job applications, hoping for a break.

Then, finally, it came—a job offer that seemed like a lifeline and the answer to my prayers. It promised stability, a regular paycheck, and an end to my financial worries. I was over the moon. No more scrambling from one temporary job to another.

But as the days passed, my excitement turned sour. The job demanded more than I had imagined. I was scheduled to work from 9 am to 6 pm Monday through Friday for a week, followed by a shift from 6 pm to 9 am the following week, with the cycle repeating itself. And that wasn't all—I also had to endure a 48-hour shift every other weekend, meaning I had to be at work for the entirety of two weekends each month. That means I was working an average of eighty-four hours a week.

Imagine spending nearly half of my life at work, with barely any time left for anything else. It felt like I was losing myself, suffocating in a job that drained me of happiness and fulfilment. This was a job I was trained for over six years to do. Imagine that.

But did I quit right away? You guess right. No, I did not leave the job. I felt trapped, like there was no way out. I found myself going back to the job day in and day out. Bills don't pay themselves, after all. So I soldiered on, day after day, paycheck after paycheck, feeling more and more like a prisoner of my own life.

I endured this unfulfilling engagement for five months, but it felt like an eternity. Could you imagine what would have happened if I had stayed for years? What would my life look like?

The reality is that I wasn't alone. So many people are stuck with jobs they hate to make ends meet. But the human spirit yearns for something more to bring them joy and fulfilment. That's why I decided to write this book—"**FIND YOUR WORK: Unlocking the Path to Impact, Fulfilment, and Worthy Compensation.**" It's a guide to discovering the work you're wired to do, the kind that fills your soul with joy and fulfilment and impacts the world around you. It's about finding fulfilment and earning a worthy reward— not just financial rewards but also the intangible rewards money can't buy.

So, if you're tired of feeling trapped in a job that drains you and craves a life of purpose and passion, then this book is for you. Let's embark on this journey together and find the work that brings joy and fulfilment to our souls because life is too short to spend doing anything less.

In today's workforce, discontent seems to be a prevailing theme, with statistics showing widespread job dissatisfaction. In 2022 alone, a staggering 60% of workers reported feeling emotionally detached at work, while 19% admitted to feeling downright miserable.[1] Moreover, a concerning 85% of individuals worldwide find themselves dissatisfied with their professional lives, highlighting the magnitude of this global issue.[2] This dissatisfaction isn't just confined to emotions; it's also impacting mental health, with job dissatisfaction linked to a 1.5-1.9 times increase in the odds of mental health problems.[3]

This shows that more people long for something more fulfilling than what their jobs offer. This is the reason for this book: It is never too late to find your work and unlock the path to impact, fulfilment, and worthy compensation.

Let us put on our seatbelt for an impactful ride.

Chapter One

WORK IS A BLESSING AND NOT A CURSE

Welcome to the first chapter of this book, *"**Find Your Work:** Unlocking the Path to Impact, Fulfilment, and Worthy Compensation"*. In this journey of self-discovery and empowerment, we are journeying to redefine our relationship and perspective with work. Contrary to popular belief, work is not a necessary evil—it is a blessing, a pathway to fulfilment, and a path to profound meaning in our lives.

The concept of work has long been intertwined with notions of struggle. From the biblical narrative of

Adam and Eve's expulsion from the Garden of Eden to modern-day tales of the daily grind, we've been conditioned to view work through a lens of hardship and toil. It's no news that God cursed man because he sinned, and it was stated that he will eat out of his struggle: *'Cursed is the ground for your sake; In toil, you shall eat of it all the days of your life.'*[4] But what if we challenged this narrative? What if we dared to see work not as a curse but as a gift and blessing—an opportunity to express our talents, reveal ourselves and gifts, contribute to the world, and cultivate a sense of purpose?

THE ORIGIN OF WORK

Let's delve into the origin of work, a narrative often overshadowed by tales of punishment and toil. We typically perceive work as stemming from man's failure to obey God. *"If Adam and Eve had not sinned, I would have been enjoying myself, eating and drinking in Eden,"* I used to think as a young boy. This sentiment is shared by many. We wish they had not disobeyed

God so that we could sleep as long as we wanted and eat anything we desired without having to work. We regard work as a consequence of their disobedience and a punishment for their transgression against the Divine. However, what if I told you that work existed before humanity disobeyed the Divine?

From the very beginning, we witness the Creator facing a chaotic earth and undertaking the task of bringing order out of the chaos. The creation story reflects the Creator at work, as it took Him six days to establish order from the earth's disorder. God worked diligently for six days, necessitating a rest on the seventh. Without such hard work, there would be no need for rest. And this occurred long before man and his disobedient act.

According to the creation story, God spoke, and those things He called into existence came into being. However, upon closer inspection, we observe that it took an entire day for some of the things He called to come into being. *"God called the light Day, and the darkness He called Night. So the evening and the morning were the first day"*[5]. If it were merely about speaking, it might not entail much work, but ensuring that what was spoken came into existence required a full day—a significant twenty-four hours. This process continued for six more days. This is undeniably work. Upon completing His work, there was a sense of fulfilment and satisfaction. *"Then God saw everything that He had made, and indeed it was very good. So the evening and the morning were the sixth day."*[6] This also demonstrates that work is not a curse but a blessing—a path to impact, fulfilment, and worthy compensation.

MAN WAS CREATED BECAUSE THERE WAS WORK FOR HIM TO DO

It is interesting to know that the creation of man was not merely an afterthought or a random occurrence but an outcome of purpose. The Divine does not embark on an endeavour without a reason or purpose in mind. Everything created, from the sun to the moon, serves a distinct purpose, and man is no exception. When He made the sun, He had it in mind for it to reign during the day by providing light, and when He created the moon, there was no exception in giving it a clear reason for its existence. The same applied to every other creation, including man.

When God was about to create man, there was an innovative meeting on what the man would do and the resources needed to get his assignment done. In fact, he is the brilliance of God's creative ability as he is an outcome of the greatest innovation ever. One of the exciting reasons for his creation was to engage in meaningful work, as until the time he was created, it was clearly stated that there was no man to work in the garden. *"Before any plant of the field was in the earth and before any herb of the field had grown. For the Lord God had not caused it to rain on the earth, and there was no man to till the ground; ... Then the Lord God took the man and put him in the garden of Eden to tend and keep it."*[7,8] This is far from the likely notion that he was placed in the garden for leisure without engaging in any work. He was not there to eat anything he liked, sleep as long as he could, and then eat again, but he was placed in the garden to take care of it. He was saddled with the responsibility of ensuring the smooth operation of the garden and earth. Essentially, he was called to be a manager. Perhaps the words 'manager' and 'management' are derived from the word 'man' – m**an**ager, m**an**agement.

We can see that work emerges not as a consequence of sin but as an intrinsic part of the creation of the human race. The first human was entrusted with the stewardship of Eden and the Earth, given the noble task of tending to its beauty and abundance. Far from being a burden, this was a call to responsibility and an invitation to co-create with God. Thus, man's purpose from the outset was not merely to indulge in idleness but to actively participate in the stewardship of creation. He wasn't there simply to satisfy his desires but to contribute to the garden's flourishing entrusted to his care.

Furthermore, it's crucial to recognise that man was created in the image and likeness of God. It was stated that *'God said, "Let Us make man in Our image, according to Our likeness; let them have dominion over the fish of the sea, over the birds of the air, and over the cattle, over all the earth and over every creeping thing that creeps on the earth.'*[9] This means that man was designed to reflect the Creator, who Himself engaged in the act of creation. The Creator's work was so demanding that He rested on the seventh day. Therefore, if man was made in the likeness of God, he must also be a creator, and creation necessitates work. **There is no meaningful creation without work.**

Work serves as the vessel for expressing our creative abilities. While one can conceive endless possibilities in the mind, it is through work that these dreams manifest into tangible realities. Without the necessary effort, creations remain intangible and are devoid of any benefit. Thus, work not only unleashes the brilliance of our creative potential but also guides us towards impact, fulfilment, and compensation.

Have you ever wondered why engaging in the right work brings a sense of fulfilment? It's because **work provides an avenue for self-expression.** Imagine living without the ability to express your innate talents—it would be like a bird grounded from flight or, a fish unable to swim or the sun unable to shine. By engaging our creative abilities and revealing our gifts and selves through meaningful work, we attain inner peace, tranquillity, and a profound sense of fulfilment of purpose. You can see that at the centre of man's existence is work to express the reason for his creation and existence.

Perhaps you're pondering on what work you are wired to do. Could it be accounting, law, medicine, or another field altogether? It could be, and it may not. I hope that is not an ambiguous answer. Here is the acid test: if your profession fails to provide uniqueness, fulfilment and an avenue for impacting others, whether you're a doctor, lawyer, or police officer, then it may simply be a job—a means of earning a living.

However, it's entirely feasible to transform your profession into more than just a source of income. You can infuse it with purpose, allowing your innate abilities and gifts to shine. Consider a teacher who not only imparts knowledge but also uplifts the downtrodden or less privileged, recognising the untapped potential in their students and guiding them toward brilliance. Or envision an artist pouring their heart into a masterpiece, creating a timeless symbol of significance. The key lesson here is to harmonise your innate gifts with your chosen profession, thereby leaving a lasting impact on the world. Doing so unlocks the path to both fulfilment and worthy compensation.

Let us consider one more thing before we conclude our discussion in this chapter. As a young boy, I have often wondered why Paul said, *"Just as He chose us in Him before the foundation of the world."*[10] I couldn't fathom how God could have chosen us before the world's creation. Did that imply we existed before the creation of the earth? Where were we if we indeed existed before God formed the earth? It wasn't until I grasped the concept of 'The two Creation' that I understood what he meant.

What is this concept all about? In his book, *"The 7 Habits of Highly Effective People,"* Stephen Covey introduces the idea of mental and physical creations. This principle illustrates that all things are created twice—first in the mind and then in the physical realm. Just as a building follows a blueprint, our physical manifestations are preceded by mental conceptions. Covey emphasises the importance of beginning with the end in mind, utilising the power of imagination to envision what we desire before bringing it into existence.

Consider, for instance, the story of an aspiring entrepreneur. Before launching a new business venture, they engage in extensive brainstorming, strategic planning, and visualisation exercises. Through this mental creation process, they clarify their goals, identify potential obstacles, and map out actionable steps toward success. Only after solidifying their vision in their mind do they proceed to the physical creation phase—drafting business plans, securing funding, and bringing their ideas to fruition.

Similarly, let's examine an artist's journey preparing to paint a masterpiece. Before touching brush to canvas, they spend time immersed in creative contemplation, envisioning the colours, shapes, and emotions they wish to convey. Through this mental creation process, they tap into their imagination, allowing their inner vision to guide their artistic expression. They translate their mental concept into physical form only after refining their mental concept, bringing their painting to life stroke by stroke.

In both examples, the power of the two creations is evident. Individuals harness the transformative potential of imagination, clarity, and intentionality by first engaging in mental creation. This process enables them to align their actions with their desires and aspirations, paving the way for greater fulfilment and success. As Covey suggests, by beginning with the end in mind, individuals can take proactive control of their lives, shaping their destiny and manifesting their dreams into reality.

As seen above, God envisioned man on earth before creating the physical world. This was why Paul claimed that He had chosen us before the foundation of the world. In fact, it was because He had us in mind and knew what He wanted us to do—to dominate on earth—that He went all the way to create the earth. If we had not come to God's mind, there would have been no reason for forming the earth and all that is in it. In other words, we gave the earth meaning, purpose and significance.

As we draw the curtain on our discussion in this chapter, it is evident that work, far from being a curse, is a blessing the Creator bestowed upon humanity. From the beginning of creation, man was designed to engage in meaningful work, reflecting the image and likeness of the Creator. Through the concept of the two creations—mental and physical—we recognise that work serves as a vehicle for expressing our creative potential and fulfilling our purpose on earth. As we continue our journey, let us carry with us the understanding that **work is not a necessary evil but an opportunity to express our innate gifts and uniqueness,** thus unlocking the path to impact, fulfilment, and worthy compensation.

Chapter Two

YOUR JOB VERSUS YOUR WORK

Contrary to popular belief, we have seen that work is a blessing, not a curse—a concept explored in detail in our last chapter. Now, let's delve deeper into the distinction between your job and your work. Are they the same, or do they represent different aspects of our lives? If indeed they are different, what sets them apart? Can one achieve great success, fortune, and fulfilment while holding a job, or is true fulfilment found aligning with one's work or maybe both? These questions, along with others, form the focal point of this chapter. Are you content with your current job, or do you yearn for something more? If you yearn for something more, how can you rewrite your narrative? Join me as we embark on this exploration, seeking clarity and understanding of the relationship between your job and your work

DON'T CONFUSE YOUR JOB WITH YOUR WORK.

Your job is a paid position—it's what you're compensated to do within the confines of your employment. **While your job provides financial sustenance, your work transcends mere employment; it encompasses what you were born to do, what ignites your passion and purpose. Your work is the intersection of your gifts, values, and calling—a manifestation of your unique contribution to the world.** You were created with a purpose, which is your work; you were not created without a reason. It is, therefore, crucial not to confuse your job with your work.

Imagine if I asked you, 'Who are you?' Would you say, 'I am an accountant' or 'I am a medical doctor'? Does that define you entirely? Are you defined solely by the profession you were trained for or the job you're paid to do? This confusion of identity often leads to depression and dejection when individuals are separated from their jobs, as they have come to define themselves by their occupation. **When you distinguish your job from your work, you'll find peace even in the face of a job loss, knowing that your unique contribution to the world—your work—cannot be taken away.** It is in-built. Being fired from your job may even serve as a signal for you to focus entirely on your work and true calling.

While your job may provide financial sustenance, your work brings a more profound sense of fulfilment and meaning, enriching both your life and the lives of others. As Frederick Buechner astutely remarked, *'Your vocation in life is where your greatest joy meets the world's greatest need.'* The vocation he referred to here is undoubtedly your work. You will discover the intersection between your greatest joy and the world's need when you can find and embrace your work.

The story of Steve Harvey vividly illustrates the distinction between "your job" and "your work". Renowned as a comedian, actor, and television host, Harvey's early career saw him as a salesman—this was his job, the role he was compensated for within the confines of his employment. Yet, deep down, he felt his true calling lay elsewhere. From the tender age of 10, Harvey harboured dreams of hosting television shows, though uncertain of how to realise them.

While working as a salesman, he would craft joke scripts and sell them for a mere ten dollars apiece. This continued for two years until he got an opportunity at a comedy club on October 8, 1985, which altered the course of his life. This opportunity allowed him to taste and embrace his work, what he was born to do, and he never looked back afterwards.

This brings the word of the great teacher to mind, *"But Jesus told him, "Anyone who puts a hand to the plow and then looks back is not fit for the Kingdom of God"*[11]

He went to drop off one of his scripts when he met Gladys. He had never heard of a comedy club until he met Gladys, who asked, 'You are the dude writing jokes for AJ?' He replied, 'Yeah.' She then exclaimed about how funny his jokes were.

Harvey was twenty-seven, and despite having written jokes, he had never heard of a comedy club until this conversation.

She then said, 'Why don't you tell the jokes yourself at the comedy club?'

'Tell the joke myself?' exclaimed Harvey.

She said, 'Yeah.'

So he thought maybe this was what he had been asking God for all his life.

So he went to the comedy club, signed up to perform the following week, and sat down to watch the comedy. Gladys bought him some chicken wings and grapefruit, as he was broke. Ten people were to perform; they came up one after the other, but Harvey did not laugh. The lady asked, 'You are not laughing at any of these jokes.'

He did not laugh because what they were doing was his actual gift—what he had been doing his whole life. He did not laugh because he knew everything they would say and what they should have said before they said it.

Now, it got to the tenth guy, and no one showed up, so they picked up the performers for the following week. 'Steve Harvey, come on up,' they called. Harvey wasn't expecting this and asked, 'Does someone got the same name I got?' The lady replied, 'You can't be stupid. It is you.' And then he went up on the stage.

When he got to the stage, he told the audience, 'I appreciate you all for clapping, but I am not supposed to be here. I am on next week's show,' and the audience laughed. How could they have laughed at such? He continued, 'Really, I have nothing for you.'

Gladys shouted, 'Tell them about when you were boxing.' On the way to the show, he had told the lady about boxing. So he did the boxing joke, and he had the audience on the floor laughing. He also made the joke he had not sold yet. That night, he won the amateur night on October 8th, 1985, and was paid 50 dollars. He got into the car, Gladys driving him home, a 40-minute drive, and he cried all the way.

'Why are you crying?' she asked, 'You just won 50 dollars.'

'You won't understand. I was just born today,' Harvey replied.

This illustrates a man who had just gotten in touch with what he was born to do—his work. He had gotten in touch with his gift and purpose.

The next day, he quit his job as a salesman, costing him his home. He became homeless and lived in his car for three years, but he did not waver as he said, 'I was born today.' He has come to terms with his work. He knew that he had always been on the job all along, and it was time for him to be on his work. Like Jacob said, *'When shall I prepare for my home?'*[12]

Despite facing numerous setbacks and challenges, Harvey never lost his passion for comedy and entertainment. He recognised that his work—his inherent gift for making people laugh and inspiring others—was his true calling and purpose. Harvey's work was the intersection of his gifts, values, and calling—a manifestation of his unique contribution to the world.

Through embracing his work, Harvey found fulfilment and success beyond measure. His perseverance and dedication eventually made him one of the most renowned figures in the entertainment industry. Harvey's story serves as a powerful reminder that while our jobs may provide financial stability, our work—our true calling—brings profound fulfilment and meaning to our lives, enriching not only ourselves but also the lives of others.

MORE THAN WHAT TO DO

We have seen that work is what you were born to do. It aligns with your purpose in life. It defines the reason for your existence, but more than what to do, work can be defined as **'to become,' 'to reveal yourself,' 'to manifest yourself.'**

So work entails who you become to do what you were called to do. You cannot do what you were called to do without first becoming someone who can do it. In the process of engaging in your work, you express who you are.

You have the ability and gift to do what the Creator created you to do on earth, but you will need to grow into this responsibility. There is a place for growth, which is the process of becoming. **Growth, in itself, is a form of work.** As it was said, *"It is not about making your first million dollars but about who you become in the process."* In the process of pursuing what you are wired and called to do, you go through the process of becoming – the growth process.

It might not be enough to stop here in defining work; it could also mean 'to reveal' or 'to manifest yourself'. Work exposes your gifts. Put in another way, work exposes you. Your true self is exposed when you identify your work and what you are called to do. In other words, you are revealed and manifested by your work. Little wonder, the great teacher said, *"You will know them by their fruits. Do men gather grapes from thornbushes or figs from thistles?"*[13]. Our world will know your uniqueness, gifts, and value when you get on your work.

Do you know that you are on a journey of self-discovery, which is the most important adventure you can embark on? You need to be introduced to yourself. Each day, you need to come to terms with a new part of yourself you haven't known. You should seek revelation into your potential and gifts. You will be wowed at what you can do as you press on in your journey of discovering yourself.

THINK BEYOND YOUR JOB

In life, it is crucial to think beyond the confines of your job description. While your job may provide financial stability and fulfil certain goals, true fulfilment often lies in aligning your work with your passion and purpose. Thinking beyond your job means transcending the limitations of routine tasks and exploring the broader possibility of impacting your world. As well articulated by Maya Angelou,

"My mission in life is not merely to survive, but to thrive; and to do so with some passion, some compassion, some humour, and some style." This statement encapsulates the essence of thinking beyond one's job—a commitment to thriving, making a difference and not just living for survival.

Some individuals only think about survival and nothing else. They never think of how they can contribute and provide value to the world – leaving the world better than they met it. They are after a stable job, which is an illusion as there is no stable and risk-free job anywhere. Anyone can be retrenched from a job at any time. If you are old enough, you would have seen that the world is in a cycle – people will lose their jobs, and at some other time, there will be plenty of jobs.

Some individuals are after earning a stable job, birthing a family, owning a car and a house and retiring on a pension before their death – this mindset is rooted in mediocrity. Instead of settling for the status quo, individuals should aspire to think beyond their present jobs and consider their lives during retirement, for instance. With advancements in medical practice and innovation, people are living longer than ever. Imagine living 25 or more years beyond retirement—will your pension be sufficient for such a prolonged period? What would you be doing for that number of years? Would life be boring or not, interesting or otherwise? It's imperative to think beyond your job and think long-term.

Thinking beyond your job requires a shift in mindset—a willingness to break free from the norm. It involves embracing uncertainty and viewing challenges as opportunities for growth and innovation. Instead of merely focusing on job security, individuals should strive to create value, pursue their passions, and make a meaningful impact on society. Imagine if Steve Jobs, Larry Page, Bill Gates had not pursued their dreams but only after job security. As Helen Keller once said, *"Life is either a daring adventure or nothing at all."* This emphasises the importance of thinking beyond your jobs – thinking beyond the to-do list thrown at you on your job. It is time to invest time in finding your work and getting to do it with all your being and ability.

Thinking beyond your job gives you a sense of purpose and fulfilment. It allows you to align your work with your values and aspirations, enabling you to lead a more purpose-driven life. When you embrace your work, you are not driven by your boss but by yourself. You are out of bed by 4 am, for instance, not because your boss mandates you to get to your job early, but because you have a dream and vision to fulfil. Going beyond the limitations of a job-centric mindset opens you to a world of possibilities and opportunities for personal and professional growth.

It would help to recognise that life is too short to settle for mediocrity. It would help if you stepped out of your comfort zone to release your gift and ability.

So, dare to dream big and work to deliver what you have dreamt, and your future self will thank you for it.

It is also essential to know that thinking beyond your job involves recognising that you are more than the sum of your daily job descriptions and tasks. It's about tapping into your innate talents, interests, and values to create a life of significance and impact. As Albert Schweitzer said, *"Success is not the key to happiness. Happiness is the key to success. If you love what you are doing, you will be successful."* These words emphasise the importance of pursuing the work that brings you joy and fulfilment and resonates with your passions.

Thinking beyond your job requires exploring new possibilities and embracing change. It means being open to opportunities that may not fit neatly into your current job description but align with your long-term goals and aspirations. Oprah Winfrey said, *"The biggest adventure you can take is to live the life of your dreams."* This mindset encourages individuals to break free from conventional career paths and forge their unique journey towards fulfilment.

I will leave you to think about what Ralph Waldo Emerson said, *"Do not go where the path may lead, go instead where there is no path and leave a trail."* This encourages you to hart your own course and leave a legacy far beyond your job title's confines.

YOUR JOB IS TEMPORARY WHILE YOUR WORK IS PERMANENT.

One way to live beyond disappointment is to understand that your job is temporary while your work is permanent. As we have seen before, your job is a means of earning a living—a role that may change over time, subject to economic conditions, industry trends, and personal circumstances. On the other hand, your work transcends the limitations of any specific job title or position; it encompasses your innate talents, passions, and purpose in life, which cannot be taken away from you.

It is wise to keep your treasure where it cannot be stolen or corrupted. As the great teacher said, *"Store your treasures in heaven, where moths and rust cannot destroy, and thieves do not break in and steal."*[14] You should invest in what cannot be taken away from you – your work. It is a wise decision to invest in yourself. Your boss cannot take this away from you. Even if you are retrenched from your job, you cannot be sacked from your work – your gifts and unique contribution to the world. Of course, that does not mean that you should not strive for excellence in your job. I will expound on "staying excellent in both your job and your work" later in this book.

Investing in refining your skills and improving your ability to express your gifts will leave the world a better place, and this is a path to creating lasting impact, fulfilment, and worthy compensation.

Imagine a fictional story of a software engineer who dedicates years to their job, only to face layoff during a company restructuring. While their job may have defined a significant part of their identity for a time, it ultimately proved transient. Despite the setback of losing their job, these individuals can still harness their programming skills and creativity to pursue new opportunities to solve real-world problems. In doing so, they transform setbacks into comebacks, embarking on a journey of impact, fulfilment, and worthy compensation, both monetarily and much more.

A concept that quickly comes to mind, which I think we should consider, is the concept of 'identity' – who we are. This concept has been a significant quest for humanity for years as we search for our true selves. We have attempted to answer questions such as: who am I? Where am I from? How did I get here? What am I supposed to do here? Among others. These questions have formed the foundation for various religions, beliefs, traditions, cultures, and scientific explanations. The concept has filled volumes of books, all in an attempt to understand our identity.

Without understanding your identity, achieving great success is unlikely. It can be likened to a fish trying to fly due to a misplaced identity.

As crucial as this concept is to our fulfilment, many individuals have tied their identity to external factors such as their profession or circumstances, leading to a skewed opinion about themselves and their capacity. Consider if you were asked, 'Who are you?' Would your response not be your job title? 'I am an accountant' or 'I am a surgeon.' A question worth pondering is, 'Does your profession define your entire being?'"

Attaching our identity to our jobs can lead to heartbreak, depression, and even suicidal attempts when we are separated from the job. This is because we have equated our being with the job. What if you understand that your job does not define who you are or what your significance is? This realisation will help you withstand any threat of losing your job. You may even see the loss of your job as an opportunity.

Richelle E. Goodrich also noted, *"Disappointment is really just a term for our refusal to look on the bright side."*

Additionally, defining ourselves solely by external outcomes—whether success or failure—only perpetuates a cycle of self-limiting beliefs and emotional turmoil. When we achieve success, we may bask in the glory of our accomplishments, labelling ourselves as "a success." However, when confronted with failure, we may internalise the setback, adopting the identity of "failure."

True self-awareness transcends such definitions of our worth based on external circumstances. Our inherent worth remains unchanged, unaffected by external events, whether positive or negative. **You are not a success because you achieve success, nor are you a failure because you experience failure. Understanding this concept is crucial as you navigate life's journey, as you will encounter both triumphs and setbacks.** Be prepared for both, knowing that they do not define you. In moments of failure, find the strength to rise and soar even higher, taking advantage of the setback just as an eagle goes for the storm. Come to think of it, without such setbacks, you may not attain the height you desire. The eagle rides on the wings of the storm to achieve incredible height. You need to know how to ride on setbacks to attain great success. Take a moment to think about this.

Imagine the story of the man born blind. He was in this state for years and was identified with his external circumstances, which do not define him. The man may also have identified himself as such. He was called the blind man. Have you considered why he was referred to as the blind man and not called by his name? Doesn't he have a name? The disciples even assumed that he was blind because his parents sinned, but Jesus identified the reason for his setback *"Jesus answered, "Neither this man nor his parents sinned, but that the works of God should be revealed in him."*[15].

Your setback does not define your identity. Instead, it was meant for your success – to express your strength, patience, and gift. You will almost always be wrong if you define yourself according to your external circumstances, either favourable or otherwise. Prophet Samuel nearly made the mistake of anointing the wrong king for Israel because he attached external features to the identity of those who presented themselves to him. We are usually more than what we are going through or what our achievements are.

The timeless story of Jesus being tempted by the devil illustrates the dangers of attaching our identity to external validation. When tempted to prove his identity by turning stones into bread, Jesus steadfastly refused, knowing that his true identity as the beloved Son of God transcended any external demonstration of power. *'Now when the tempter came to Him, he said, "If You are the Son of God, command that these stones become bread.'*[16] This was just after 40 days when God declared that He was His beloved Son, 'And suddenly a voice came from heaven, saying, *"This is My beloved Son, in whom I am well pleased."*'[17] Whether Jesus turned the stone into bread or not, it does not change his identity as the son of God. You are who you are, irrespective of what is going on. All you need to do is express your gifts to benefit the world, not to prove your identity.

That was just a quick insight into the concept of "identity." Don't forget that we are considering what could stand the test of time, your job or your work. The impermanence of a job is evident in today's rapidly changing labour market, where industries evolve, and new technologies disrupt traditional roles. In such a dynamic environment, individuals must cultivate resilience and adaptability, recognising that a job loss does not define their worth or potential. As Henry Ford once said, *"Failure is simply the opportunity to begin again, this time more intelligently."* This quote underscores the importance of resilience and learning from setbacks, turning adversity into opportunity.

Conversely, your work—the essence of who you are and what you are meant to contribute to the world—is enduring and timeless. It reflects your unique combination of talents, experiences, and values, shaping your identity and influencing your impact on others. While a job may provide financial security and stability in the short term, your work leaves a lasting legacy and stability.

As much as you want to release your gift and contribute to improving the world, you shouldn't settle for mediocrity on your job. Even within the confines of your employment, your aim should be to pursue excellence and find ways to impact those around you positively. Strive for excellence in all your endeavours. Why hesitate if further education or training is necessary to enhance your professional skills? Take the initiative to expand your knowledge and become indispensable in your field. Avoid being the first in line for dismissal at the slightest opportunity. Instead, position yourself as a valuable asset that your institution or company cannot afford to lose. Consider the scenario where your employer offers to double your salary and provide additional perks to retain your services, recognising the significant value you bring. Commit to continuous learning by dedicating each day to acquiring new knowledge and skills relevant to your profession. Remember, the moment you cease learning, you gradually diminish value.

Another crucial aspect to consider is staying abreast of trends and changes in your field of expertise. Some shifts can disrupt and render a profession obsolete. I can recall learning to type on a typewriter, the distinctive sound of each keystroke resonating in my memory. The typewriter was once a vital tool for many professionals, but it was replaced by new technology over time. Today, we have desktop computers, laptops, and various other devices.

Imagine someone who failed to update their skills, clinging solely to typewriter proficiency. It would spell disaster, wouldn't it? The same holds true for numerous other professions. Tasks that once took hours or days can now be completed in seconds with technological advancements, rendering some jobs redundant. I recall scenes from a movie where complex calculations were painstakingly performed on large boards, with individuals climbing ladders to work across the board's surface. Such roles were once paid positions. However, with the advent of computers, these tasks can be completed in minutes without needing boards, ladders, or additional salaries.

DO NOT BE QUICK TO FORGET THAT YOU ARE A STEWARD

We quickly forget our responsibility as stewards, and to make it worse, we do not even remember that we are stewards in the first place. How can we act as we ought to if we do not know ourselves or our roles? It is akin to the story of a lion taken as a cub by a hunter and raised among sheep. Though the lion grew strong, it never saw itself as a lion but as a sheep and behaved accordingly. This highlights the concept of identity. Do not forget that you were not a result of chance but of intentionality in the mind of God, and His purpose was for you to be a steward and manager.

Who is a steward? A steward can be referred to as a resource manager, someone entrusted to care for a property or an individual entrusted with resources saddled with the responsibility to keep, invest, and multiply them.

The Creator is a businessman; like any businessman, He desires to increase and profit. When He created the birds, He clearly instructed them: *"Be fruitful and multiply."*[18] This directive wasn't exclusive to the birds; it extended to other animals, sea creatures, plants, and, most importantly, mankind. He explicitly instructed humans to be fruitful, multiply, replenish, subdue, and have dominion over the earth. This is a call to take the role of a businessman and a call to stewardship and responsibility.

When we fail to turn our gifts into fruits, we are not following the instructions the Creator gave us because He said, *"Be fruitful."*[19] Our gifts can be likened to seeds that need to be planted, nurtured, and cultivated into fruits that benefit us and others. It's no coincidence that God didn't start the instruction by saying, "Be seedful." He has already provided the seeds—the resources we need to be fruitful. He has called us to steward these resources for profit and increase.

There are steps and processes involved in a seed becoming a fruit. A farmer understands this well; they prepare the soil before planting the seed, ensuring it is suitable for growth. If the soil isn't conducive, the seed may not germinate or could wither soon after sprouting. The story of the Sower illustrates this vividly: some seeds fell on the roadside and were eaten by birds, some on rocky ground and sprouted but withered due to lack of proper roots, others among thorns were choked, but those on fertile soil yielded abundant increase. Even among the seeds that fell on good soil, some multiplied by thirty, some by sixty, and some by a hundred. Soil preparation is crucial for seed growth.

You need to provide the right environment for your seed's growth. Don't let negative thoughts or distractions like social media and movies choke your gift. Your mind is the soil for your seed; prepare it well. It's no wonder Solomon, in his wisdom, advised, *"Guard your heart with all diligence, for out of it spring the issues of life."*[20]

This is just one step in turning your seed into fruit. If this is just a step, you could see that turning your seed or gift into fruit or finished products requires diligence and commitment. Besides preparing the soil, you must plant the seed, nurture it, protect it from weeds, pests, and insects, and then wait patiently. Many seek shortcuts, wanting instant results, but growing your gifts to fruition takes patience, perseverance, and consistency—that's your work.

The story of the grass and the bamboo is a powerful illustration of patience, consistency, and their eventual rewards. When you plant grass seeds, it sprouts within a week or so. It grows quickly, reaching its full height in a matter of weeks. However, once it peaks, it remains relatively unchanged and withers quickly. On the other hand, when you plant bamboo seeds, you water and nurture them, but nothing seems to happen for the first year or even the second, third and fourth year. It requires consistent care and attention without any visible signs of progress.

Yet, in the fifth year, something remarkable occurs. The bamboo shoots begin to emerge, and within just a few weeks, they can grow up to 80 feet tall. This sudden growth isn't because the bamboo suddenly grew fast; it's because it spent the first few years establishing a robust underground root system. This story teaches us that our efforts may not yield immediate results like the bamboo. We may need to patiently nurture our skills, gifts, relationships, or endeavours without seeing visible progress. But if we remain consistent and steadfast in our efforts, the rewards will eventually manifest, often in ways beyond our imagination. Just as the bamboo's growth astonishes those who witness it, our perseverance and dedication will lead to extraordinary outcomes.

Remember, people are attracted to your fruit, not your seed. They are interested in what they would gain from you. When Jesus walked the earth, people were all over him, not out of love for Him but because they desired the benefits He offered. They travelled far and endured hardships, even travelling through the night to obtain the fruit of His ministry.

Ultimately, people will pay you for what they can gain from you—your fruit. So, be fruitful.

Before concluding that you haven't been given anything to manage or care for, consider the resources the Creator has entrusted you for stewardship. It's up to you to convert these resources into valuable fruits and products. What are the resources He has given us to profit from?

Here are some of the resources God has given you to nurture and profit from:

> 1. **Your time.** He has given you time on Earth. This resource is distributed equally to everyone, regardless of age, gender, or status. Each one of us has twenty-four hours a day to invest. Unfortunately, many squander this precious resource on unproductive activities. Some liken time to money, a comparison with some truth, as time is not just money but life itself. Every moment spent, whether watching a movie or engaging in meaningful endeavours like writing a book, is engaging in a transaction which could be a good or bad investment.

When you watch a free movie or scroll through pages on the internet for free, it's not free because you paid for it - you paid with your time. Time is a form of currency. By reading this book, for instance, you are investing your time in gaining valuable information and engaging in a productive pursuit and investment which would yield dividends. The next time you engage in an activity, ask yourself if it is worth the time you are paying for it. If it does, continue with the activity; if it does not, you know what to do.

2. **Your mind.** Our minds are among the most potent resources bestowed upon us by the Creator. The mind determines our trajectory in life, shaping who we become and what we achieve. Therefore, paying close attention to this resource and capitalising on its potential is essential. I am writing a book on harnessing the power of the mind, which I

regard as the richest mine on Earth. You may want to read the book when it is ready.

3. **Your attention.** This is equally crucial. Consider that everyone vies for your attention. Its sought-after nature signifies its value. Advertisements, social media content, salespersons, and marketers all compete for your attention, while you may not even realise the significance of this resource. You must know how to focus your attention on productive work and activity.

4. **Your relationships.** This is another resource you need to nurture, which is crucial to your growth and success. We do not live in isolation. You need people—like-minded individuals and those who have gone beyond you—to help you unleash your gifts upon the world. Your immediate family should also be prioritised as you journey toward profiting with your gift.

5.   **Your unique abilities and gifts.** There are no two people on Earth who are the same, not even identical twins; they have traits that differentiate them. I believe that's why we all have unique fingerprints, showing that we possess exceptional abilities and gifts that can benefit the world. No one else can offer the world what you have in the same way you can, so it's crucial to identify your unique abilities and gifts and use them to make the world a better place. You are called to steward these unique abilities and gifts. What would you do with them? Would you profit and bless the world with them, hide them, or abuse them?

It is also crucial that I emphasise that God is a businessman. Many people do not align with this concept of the Creator. They are willing to go to heaven as an escape plan without considering that this isn't the primary reason they are on Earth - they have got to profit the kingdom they long to go to.

Imagine you are a businessman and invested in a business, say a million dollars. You have a manager to manage the money and any other resources you have put into building the business into a profitable company. What do you expect from the manager? Of course, you expect the manager to increase the returns on investment. When you request an annual return or find out how the business has done for the past year, you realise that the manager has done nothing. How would you feel? And what would you do? Or, to make it worse, the one million dollars you invested in the business has been depleted to one hundred thousand dollars. What would be your response to this?

This demonstrates what many individuals are doing. The Creator has invested millions of dollars worth of resources in them, but they do not profit from the investment. Do you think the Creator wouldn't ask about how you managed His investment when you show up to Him?

There is a story that illustrates the Creator, where He gave His servants money to do business until He returned. *'So he called ten of his servants, delivered to them ten minas, and said to them, "Do business till I come."'*[21] I love how the New International Version puts it: *'So he called ten of his servants and gave them ten minas. "Put this money to work," he said, "until I come back."'*[22] You have got to put your gifts to work.

WHILE ON YOUR JOB.

My mum would say, *'The way you do another person's work is the way you will do yours.'* She used this to emphasise that whatever task we undertake, even for someone else, we should do it excellently as if it were our own. This is a concept we cannot overlook.

Seeking your work doesn't mean you should drop your job or become redundant. If you have a job, you can continue with it until you feel compelled to leave it for your true calling. You may not have to leave your job, as it may align with your work, simultaneously allowing you to excel in both. We've seen people who excel in both their job and their calling, and that's the focus of this section — how to thrive in your job while pursuing your true work.

Before we delve into what you should do while on your job, let's consider what you stand to gain by excelling in your current position. As the great teacher mentioned, *'And if you have not been trustworthy with someone else's property, who will give you property of your own?'*[23] Isn't this about being a steward or manager? If you are not responsible for another person's business or work, how can you expect to succeed with your own?

It resonates with the law of giving — you receive what you give. If you exhibit 'unfaithfulness, a carefree attitude, among other negative traits' in your job, that is likely what you'll encounter in your work. Consider this scenario: if you're consistently late in submitting projects at your job, you'll probably struggle with timeliness in your personal endeavours because you've formed a habit of completing tasks untimely. Thus, it's crucial to cultivate positive habits while working for others, as these habits will benefit you when you pursue your work. Interestingly, whatever you do for another person indirectly impacts you.

Reflecting on my own experience, I recall leading a team tasked with creating weekly bible studies while in school. I approached this responsibility as if it were my own. We embraced innovation and compiled the studies into a comprehensive manual, developing lessons for the entire semester. This dedication often meant sacrificing my breaks to stay back at school while others went home. Little did I realise I was investing in myself. While serving, I learned valuable lessons and acquired various skills along the way. For instance, I learned to type without looking at the keyboard, a skill I now use regularly. When I type, sometimes people ask how I learned to do it, and interestingly, I picked it up along the way without planning to. This is just one of several skills I picked while serving in the position. What's remarkable is that these skills are mine for life — no one can take them away from me. While the paycheck from a job may eventually be spent, the knowledge and skills gained while on your job are invaluable and enduring. Therefore, it's essential to focus not only on your salary but also on what you can learn - ensuring you acquire assets that no one can take from you. And do not forget that learning comes with doing.

There was once a young man destined to be a leader, called to guide his family and nation through famine. His work was to save nations from hunger. Despite knowing his calling, he found himself on a job far from home, serving as a mere servant. Before he got himself far from home, he had always enjoyed preferential treatment from his father.

Despite being aware of his destiny, he didn't abandon his job or wallow in self-pity while serving his master. Instead, he excelled in his role, catching the attention of his master, who eventually promoted him to head the team of workers. He became successful as an employee, laying the foundation for his future leadership. Had he not demonstrated excellence, he wouldn't have been promoted, nor would he have had the opportunity to lead. Leading the team allowed him to develop crucial leadership skills, an invaluable asset for future endeavours. Essentially, he was already crafting his CV through his exemplary performance. This story teaches us the importance of starting our work from our current job and giving our best in everything we do.

This young man's success did not last long, as he was implicated in a terrible act that landed him in prison. Life's journey is not always smooth; there will be ups and downs along the way. We must learn to manage life's blows and not lose our heads as we journey towards expressing our gifts.

While in prison, he didn't withdraw into himself but took the initiative to improve the prison's environment. Soon, the prison wardens took note of his impact. You may need to go beyond your job description to enhance your organisation. By doing so, you will distinguish yourself. Can you dedicate an extra hour to impactful activities that could increase your company's revenue, close a deal, or refine a project? Brian Tracy recounted how he saved his company from a deal that could have cost them millions of dollars by putting in extra effort and conducting thorough research. He wasn't indifferent; he approached the transaction as if it were his own.

This young man persisted until his work was recommended to the king for his service. He did not disappoint his recommender but lived up to the expectations. This ushered him into his calling and work. I'm referring to no other than Joseph and his journey to Egypt, where he played a crucial role in helping the nation survive the famine.

Now let us look at some of the things you should do while you are on your job:

1. **Seek To Improve Yourself:** While on a job, continuously seeking self-improvement is essential. Take advantage of any training opportunities, whether attending workshops, enrolling in courses, reading books related to your profession or participating in seminars. For example, imagine a sales representative who consistently attends sales training programs and reads books on sales techniques. Over time, this individual will become a top performer in the company, consistently exceeding sales targets and getting better along the way

2. **Refine Your Skills:** Another crucial aspect of excelling in your job is to refine your skills continually. Whether you're in a position as a medical doctor, lawyer, software developer, marketer, or accountant, staying abreast of industry trends and advancements is essential. Disruptive innovations are coming up daily,

which may threaten your job, so you need to stay updated and refine your skills to meet these new trends. Take the initiative to learn new technologies and techniques relevant to your field. Additionally, seek opportunities to apply your skills in different contexts and projects, as this will help you gain a deeper understanding and mastery of your craft.

3. **Own The Business:** While you may not own the company, adopting an ownership mentality can significantly impact your performance and contributions. Take ownership of your responsibilities and projects, treating them as your business ventures. This mindset fosters accountability, initiative, and a sense of pride in your job. Furthermore, look for opportunities to innovate and embrace a problem-solving attitude.

4. **Be An Intrapreneur:** As an employee, you can adopt an entrepreneurial mindset within the confines of your organisation by becoming an intrapreneur. This means taking initiative, identifying opportunities for growth or improvement, and implementing innovative solutions within your role or department. Intrapreneurs are proactive problem solvers unafraid to challenge the status quo. They propose new ideas to drive the company forward. They take calculated risks, seize opportunities, and demonstrate a strong sense of ownership and accountability for their actions. For instance, consider a marketing associate who identifies a gap in the market for a new product line and pitches a marketing strategy to the organisation's management. By taking on the role of an intrapreneur, this individual contributes to the company's growth and likewise showcases and refines their leadership and strategic thinking skills.

5. **Be Innovative:** Innovation is crucial for staying ahead in today's rapidly changing business landscape. While on your job, be innovative by generating creative ideas, experimenting with new approaches, and embracing a willingness to embrace change, adaptation and evolution. Look for ways to streamline processes, improve efficiency, and enhance the customer experience through innovative solutions. At a recent conference, the entrepreneur speaker shared how one of their products contributed over 70 per cent of their total annual sales. One day, on his way home, he noticed a changing trend regarding the product. Upon returning to work, he informed his team that innovation was necessary to avoid going out of business. The team then re-strategised, and after about five years, the product sales dropped from 70 per cent to almost zero per cent. Had they not innovated, they would have faced the risk of

going out of business and being forced to merely react to the disruptive change.

6. **Think Ahead:** While focusing on your current role in your position, it is crucial to think ahead and anticipate future challenges and opportunities. Take a proactive approach to your career development by setting clear goals and objectives, both short-term and long-term. Continuously assess your skills, strengths, and areas for improvement to ensure you remain relevant in your field. Additionally, stay informed about industry trends, market developments, and technological advancements that may impact your role or industry in the future. By thinking ahead and planning strategically, you can confidently position yourself for success and navigate changes. A good example is the speaker who shared his story, which was narrated previously.

7. **Be Selfless:** Being selfless in the workplace involves prioritising the needs and well-being of others above your interests. It means going above and beyond your job description to support your colleagues, assist customers, and contribute to the overall success of the team or organisation. Practice empathy and compassion by actively listening to the concerns and challenges of others and offering support and assistance whenever possible. Be willing to share your knowledge, expertise, and resources with others to help them grow and succeed. A selfless attitude fosters a positive work environment.

These are just a few of the things you should embrace while you are on your job. Try them, and you will be glad you did.

TURN YOUR JOB INTO AN OPPORTUNITY WHERE YOU ARE PAID TO LEARN.

Turn your job into an opportunity where you are paid to learn. As Oprah Winfrey said, *"The greatest discovery of all time is that a person can change his future by merely changing his attitude."* Instead of viewing your job solely as a means to earn a paycheck, consider it a platform for growth. Approach each task and responsibility with a curious and open mindset, seeking to acquire new knowledge, skills, and experiences along the way. Treat every challenge and obstacle as a chance to learn and develop rather than a setback. Take advantage of training programs, workshops, and mentorship opportunities offered by your employer to enhance your expertise and broaden your skill set. Embrace feedback and constructive criticism as valuable learning opportunities, using them to identify areas for improvement and refine your capabilities.

Your Job Is Your Career, While Your Work Is Your Life Assignment.

Your job represents your career and what you are paid to do, while your work embodies your life assignment and what you were born to do. It's crucial not to confuse the two. Your career may earn you a paycheck, reflecting what you're trained to do, but true fulfilment comes from engaging in your life assignment. This is where you impact others profoundly and find deep personal fulfilment.

Going to college may not necessarily lead you to your life assignment; it may only end up training you for a job. Typically, the educational system prepares you for employment, while life prepares you for what you are born to do. This doesn't discourage you from pursuing education but emphasizes the importance of aligning with your life's work by leveraging your education, just as Paul excelled in his life assignment by harnessing his education and writing more than half of the New Testament books. Imagine if he hadn't been highly educated; he wouldn't have excelled as much, and we might have missed out on some profound insights he shared. While many people seek employment, you should strive to be deployed, that is, to release your gifts to create meaningful and valuable products.

You Can Retire From Your Job But Not Your Work.

Have you ever considered individuals who, even at 80 or older, are still agile and engaged in what they love to do? For these individuals, their pursuits have transcended the confines of a mere job; they've become the very definition of a life assignment. Their happiness and contentment stem from their work, which remains a source of fulfilment even in their later years.

During my time in medical school, we had a professor who, at every opportunity, longed to teach us. He was always willing to teach, going as far as organising classes on weekends when most would have taken time off. His dedication never ceased to amaze me. It was clear that what he was doing went beyond the duties of a job; it was a calling—a lifelong endeavour to impact others with his knowledge and passion. Even if he were to retire from his formal position, I have no doubt he would continue to pursue his passion, regardless of monetary compensation. This illustrates that while you may retire from a job, you never truly retire from your life's work.

If you find yourself engaged in an activity and pondering when you can retire from it, chances are it's not your true life's work. Genuine work is more than just a job; it's a calling—a lifelong commitment to a purpose greater than oneself. **Those who have discovered their life's work often find themselves shielded from depression or emptiness upon retirement, as they have found meaning and fulfilment in their endeavours.** Indeed, there is no greater encouragement than finding purpose and fulfilment in your work.

While you may leave behind the routine of a career, your life's purpose, your true calling, transcends the confines of retirement. **Retirement marks the conclusion of one chapter in your professional journey, but it doesn't signify the end of your contribution to the world.**

Retiring from a job might entail stopping job-related tasks, but it presents an opportunity to dedicate more time and energy to your life's work. Whether it's pursuing creative endeavours, volunteering, mentoring the next generation, or engaging in philanthropic activities, retirement offers the freedom to focus on what truly matters to you. It's a chance to align your actions more closely with your deepest passions and aspirations, unfettered by the demands of a traditional career. Retirement opens the door to a new chapter of purpose-driven living, where the pursuit of fulfilment takes precedence over the pursuit of a paycheck.

Your work, your life's calling, remains integral to your identity. It's the essence of who you are, reflecting your unique talents, values, and contributions to the world. Embrace retirement as an opportunity to redefine your relationship with work, allowing your passion and purpose to guide you toward new avenues of growth, fulfilment, and service to others. After all, retirement isn't the end of your journey—it's the beginning of a new chapter in which your life's work continues to unfold and inspire others long into the future.

You Can Be Fired From Your Job But Not Your Work.

Your job may be subject to fluctuations in the economy, the decisions of employers, or even changes in technology, leaving you vulnerable to termination. However, your life's work transcends these external factors; it's an intrinsic part of who you are and what you're meant to contribute to the world. While a job may be temporary or dependent upon various circumstances, your work endures.

Even if you face setbacks or unexpected changes in your employment status, your work remains – you can be fired from your job but not your work. **Losing a job can be disheartening and challenging, but it doesn't diminish the significance of your life's work.** Moments of adversity often catalyse personal growth and a renewed focus on your true calling. Being fired from a job may close one door, but it can open opportunities to realign with your life's work and pursue avenues that align more closely with your passions and values. **Your work is not bound by the constraints of corporate structures or job descriptions; it's an expression of your unique talents, aspirations, and contributions to the world.**

YOUR GIFT MAKES ROOM FOR HIM

As we draw the curtain on our discussion in this chapter, I would like to highlight the wisdom of Solomon: *"A man's gift makes room for him, and brings him before great men."*[24] Your gift creates opportunities for you and grants you access to influential figures. As I've mentioned, people are often interested in what they can gain from you. If you don't have anything valuable to offer, you may not attract the attention of prominent individuals. Joseph's time in prison was overturned, and he was brought before the king because the king valued his expertise — his gift paved the way for him and brought him into the presence of great leaders. You may want to identify your gift, hone it, and share it with the world. By doing so, you'll carve out a place for yourself, and influential individuals will seek your service.

We have come to the conclusion of this chapter. Your dedication to your success is evident in your commitment to reading this far, and I commend you for it. In the next chapter, we'll explore how you can excel both in your job and your life's work — you don't have to sacrifice one for the other. See you!

Chapter Three

EXCEL BOTH IN YOUR JOB AND YOUR LIFE'S WORK

In life's journey, we often find ourselves at a crossroads between our professional obligations and our deeper calling—the distinction between our job and our life's work. While our job may provide financial stability, our life's work encompasses our passion, purpose, and contribution to the world. This chapter delves into the art of excelling in both realms, emphasising that success in one does not necessitate sacrificing the other. Instead, it encourages a harmonious balance, where proficiency in our job complements the pursuit of our life's work and vice versa. Through practical insights and actionable strategies, we will explore how to navigate this dual path with diligence, integrity, and fulfilment.

BEFORE YOU QUIT YOUR JOB

If you asked me whether you should quit your job for your life's work right now, I may not be able to provide a definitive yes or no answer, as it largely depends on your circumstances. You need to carefully consider some factors before making such a significant decision. While this chapter primarily focuses on excelling in both your job and your life's work simultaneously, it's essential to acknowledge that for some individuals, taking the bold step of leaving their current job might be necessary to attain the fullness of their purpose on earth.

I understand the appeal of the notion of burning the bridges behind you so you can wholeheartedly pursue the goal ahead. While there's merit in such a decision, exercising wisdom in your decision-making process is equally important to avoid unnecessary hardship and experience. Having walked in your shoes before, I've experienced firsthand the toll of being trapped in a job that drains one's life and energy, leaving you unhappy and unfulfilled. That's precisely why we're delving into this topic. Now, let's explore some factors that could guide you toward reaching the best decision for yourself. Here are five questions for you.

1. Are you simply on a job or feeling enslaved by it?

I once found myself on a job where I felt enslaved. As a young professional with a family to support, I searched tirelessly for employment until I finally landed this job after numerous applications. While the job offer initially seemed like a relief, I soon realised that the demands of the position were not what I had anticipated. I worked tirelessly, spending an average of eighty-four hours a week on the job.

Eventually, I felt drained and unfulfilled, with little time to pursue meaningful activities outside the job. I felt enslaved by the job, leaving me empty and unfulfilled with no time to engage in what gave me a sense of meaning and fulfilment. My family life suffered as I returned home exhausted and seeking to catch some rest, barely able to spend quality time with them before it was time to return to the job.

Many others likely find themselves in similar situations, trapped in jobs that offer nothing beyond a paycheck but leave them empty without a sense of fulfilment and impact. From the very first month, I had wanted to leave the job. Despite my desire to leave, I felt compelled to stay due to financial obligations and the pressure of bills that needed to be paid. After enduring five months at this job, I finally decided to quit. Imagine if I had been on the job for five years or more. I cannot just imagine what it would be like.

If you find yourself in an enslaving job, it's important to consider quitting. Remaining in such a position can diminish your happiness and fulfilment, ultimately leaving you empty and unfulfilled in your purpose. Those roles can consume the time you need to identify and cultivate your unique gifts and calling.

Individuals who remain in such jobs often experience feelings of being used and trapped and may even suffer from poor mental health. It's crucial to avoid finding yourself in such a situation, as life is too short to live as a slave to your job. The creator desires us to live fulfilling and joyful lives where each day is embraced as an opportunity to pursue what brings us true happiness.

Have you heard of the boiling frog syndrome before? It's a fascinating 19th-century science experiment. Researchers found that when they put a frog in a pan of boiling water, it quickly jumped out. However, when they placed a frog in tepid water and gradually increased the temperature over time, the frog stayed and kept adjusting until it was boiled to death. The hypothesis is that the temperature change is so gradual that the frog doesn't realise it's boiling to death.[25] Similarly, instead of continually adjusting to a job that enslaves you, you must take action to avoid being trapped in an unfavourable cycle for life with its inherent effects.

2. Is your job an opportunity to get paid to learn?

This is the second factor you must consider in assessing whether quitting your job is wise- is your job an opportunity to get paid to learn? Evaluating if your current role offers the chance to acquire valuable skills and knowledge is crucial. Your job can serve as a platform for personal and professional growth, providing opportunities to learn new skills, including leadership and soft skills, gain industry insights, and increase your networks of valuable relationships. Consider if your current job provides hands-on projects which could enhance your learning of new skills or sharpen your previously learnt skills. This will allow you to get paid while honing your skills and picking up other valuable traits. Also, consider if your current position offers training programs, workshops, or mentorship opportunities that can enhance your abilities and contribute to your long-term goals and aspirations.

We've witnessed individuals who served in various positions before transitioning full-time into their calling and life's work. Serving in those roles allowed them to learn, acquire skills, and develop traits that proved invaluable in the future, all while being compensated for their engagement. Therefore, before quitting your job, it's essential to evaluate if the timing is right and if your current position offers learning opportunities that align with your life's goals and vision.

Previously, we examined Joseph's life, in which he navigated through different roles before ascending to the position of prime minister in Egypt. Despite facing challenges, Joseph remained dedicated to his duties, seizing opportunities to take on leadership responsibilities while serving. These experiences equipped him with essential skills and prepared him for the significant responsibility of leading a nation.

Hence, consider this before you quit your job. Now, let's delve into the third factor.

3. Is Your Work Embedded in Your Job?

Here is the third factor you may need to consider before quitting your current position: Is your work embedded in your job? This is because some people have found their work within their jobs. They have discovered what they were born to do within their job roles and have found ways to impact others using their jobs as a platform.

An example that comes to mind is Daniel and his friends. The government trained them for specific jobs or positions. Excelling in their studies, they began working for the government. However, while on their jobs, they demonstrated exceptional qualities that gave meaning to their lives. They became achievers and problem solvers for the country, representing their people and God well. Instead of quitting their jobs, they found a way to align their purpose with their responsibilities. So, it's essential to ask yourself: Is your work embedded in your job? Can your job provide a platform for amplifying your work?

Consider whether your current role allows you to engage in tasks that resonate with your more profound sense of fulfilment and contribute to your long-term goals. Reflect on whether your job provides opportunities for personal growth, skill development, and meaningful contributions to your field or community. Assessing the extent to which your work is intertwined with your job involves evaluating the alignment between your responsibilities and your aspirations. Can you leverage your strengths and your unique abilities in your current position? Do you feel a sense of purpose and fulfilment in your daily tasks? Additionally, consider whether your job allows you to make a positive impact on others, whether it's through serving clients, mentoring colleagues, or contributing to societal progress. Identifying areas where your work intersects with your job can help clarify whether your current role is conducive to your overall sense of fulfilment and growth.

4. Is your current position a step towards fulfilling your life's work?

Before quitting your job, here's another point to consider: Is your current role a stepping stone towards your life's work? Some individuals later discovered that their jobs were essential experiences for fulfilling their purpose on earth. Without staying in those positions, they wouldn't have learned what was necessary for their life's purpose.

As we've discussed previously, Joseph's journey can be likened to transitioning through various job positions until reaching his life's destiny. If he hadn't stayed in those roles, he wouldn't have been recommended to the king in the first place. Along the way, he undoubtedly acquired leadership skills and other valuable attributes that benefited him as a leader in a foreign land. The lesson here is that if you're currently in a job, give it your all because you're preparing the groundwork for your future success.

Before deciding to quit your job, asking yourself if your current position is a step towards fulfilling your life's purpose is essential. Don't make such a decision without careful consideration.

5. Is your work demanding your full time and attention?

Before quitting your job, here's another point to consider: Is your work demanding your full time and attention?

You can be on a job while also pursuing your life's assignment. However, there may come a time when your work grows to a point where it requires all your time and focus. In such a scenario, you'll need to leave your job to dedicate yourself entirely to your life's purpose. You'll recognise it when you get to this juncture.

When you leave your job at this stage, it's not because you want more free time or relaxation. Instead, it's because your work demands your time, energy, and focus. Several people have gotten to this point, and when they do, they know it and do not hesitate to make the right decision.

SECRET TO EXCELLING BOTH IN YOUR JOB AND YOUR LIFE'S WORK

The Wisdom of Solomon regarding your job and work is profound, as seen here: *"Sow your seed in the morning, and at evening let your hands not be idle, for you do not know which will succeed, whether this or that, or whether both will do equally well."*[26]

The principle of sowing seeds is profound because you cannot experience an increase without learning how to sow seeds - to invest your resources. The seed has the capacity to multiply itself when given the right environment and conditions. You are meant to sow your seed and not consume it. If you consume your seed, you risk having no return on investment. The wise person learns to maximise the potential of their seeds.

To sow your seed doesn't necessarily mean planting literal seeds in the ground, though it could include that. Essentially, it means investing your resources, energy, and time. So, when it's said to sow your seed in the morning, it means getting to work early. Every morning you wake up should be seen as an opportunity to invest your time, resources, attention, and gifts. If you have a job, then it's time to dive into your tasks during the day. Don't slack off during the day; approach your responsibilities to make progress, invest in yourself, and accomplish your daily goals.

It's no secret that successful people are often early risers. While others are still asleep, they're already strategising and planning their day. They start their day with positive affirmations and put their hands to work, staying productive throughout the day. So, from now on, don't waste your mornings and days. Invest your time wisely because you'll undoubtedly see a return on your investment.

You might have thought that when you finish your job for the day, it's time to relax in front of the television or enjoy a meal with your friends. However, it's clearly stated that you shouldn't let your hands be idle in the evening. This means that when you return from your job, it's time to focus on your life's work. The evening is an opportunity for personal growth and investment in your life goals and future. Instead of watching a movie, invest the time in what you were born to do.

You have dedicated your time to your employer during the day; now that is evening, it is time to devote time to yourself – it is time to invest in yourself. By doing so, you're sowing seeds both in the morning and evening. Take inspiration from the biblical figure Jacob, who asked, *"When shall I provide for my own house?"*[12] After serving his master for many years, he couldn't wait to invest in himself. You don't have to wait until retirement to invest in your life goals and yourself. When you return from your job, dive into your work. This is the secret to excelling in both your job and your life's work.

For instance, if you're an accountant, but your life goal is to help and educate children, evenings could be a valuable time to invest in such endeavours. Whether writing children's books, creating educational content for children, or other tasks aligning with your vision could be done in the evening. These efforts can be pursued alongside your job. Instead of quitting your job altogether, the solution might be to sow seeds in the morning and continue working on your passion projects in the evening.

If you're inclined to focus solely on your life's work, then dedicate both mornings and evenings to it. However, consider some factors discussed earlier before deciding to quit your job. Quitting isn't the right path for everyone, and timing is crucial when making such an important decision.

It's understandable if you're concerned about finding time for rest amidst working both morning and evening. However, there's always a way to manage it. You can carve out a few hours to invest in yourself between the end of your job and the start of your evening work. This hinges on effective time management skills. I've written a book titled "**From Overwhelmed to Organized: A Time Management Blueprint for Busy Professionals,**" which offers strategies to stay on top of your tasks and maximise your time. You can find it here [https://www.amazon.com/dp/B0BSVHBLFV].

Interestingly, we waste more time than we could imagine when we aren't intentional about our time.

Let's revisit the wisdom of Solomon: *"Sow your seed in the morning, and at evening let your hands not be idle, for you do not know which will succeed, whether this or that, or whether both will do equally well."*[26] Investing both in your job and your life's work gives you leverage. Even if you later transition to focusing full-time on your life's work, you'll realise that your investment in your job wasn't in vain if you pay attention to the previously shared wisdom about what you should do while on your job.

Now that we've explored "Excel Both In Your Job And Your Life's Work," let's dive into another chapter centred on simple steps to identify your life's work.

Chapter Four

SIMPLE STEPS TO IDENTIFYING YOUR WORK

Discovering your life's work is crucial for positively impacting the world with your gifts and attaining fulfilment. However, this task can seem daunting, leaving many feeling lost or uncertain about where to begin. Fortunately, there are simple steps we can take to identify our work and align ourselves with our true calling.

We do not have the whole time in the world to do everything, but we have enough to do the essential

tasks that align with our life goals and destiny. Therefore, you need to identify these goals.

Self-reflection is vital in identifying what you are born to do. Take the time to introspect and explore what truly excites and motivates you. Consider your passions, interests, and values. What activities ignite a sense of purpose within you? Reflecting on your past experiences can also provide valuable insights into what resonates with you more deeply.

Also, pay attention to moments of flow and fulfilment. Notice when you feel completely absorbed and engaged in an activity, losing track of time in the process. These moments often indicate alignment with your natural talents and interests. Whether it's writing, problem-solving, or helping others, identifying these flow states can point you toward your true work.

It is also essential to be open-minded along the way because sometimes your life's work may not reveal itself immediately, and that's okay. Embrace the journey of self-discovery and allow yourself to try new things. Take on different projects, volunteer for things you care about, or pursue hobbies that intrigue you. Through exploration, you may stumble upon unexpected opportunities that lead you closer to your true calling.

DISCOVER THE 3 MOST IMPORTANT GOALS IN YOUR LIFE: A QUICK AND EASY GUIDE

This is a quick and easy guide to identifying the three most important goals in your life:

1. Get a pen and a notepad.

2. Make a list of what truly excites and motivates you and what ignites a sense of purpose within you. This includes activities that align with your natural talents and interests, which get you absorbed and engaged to the point where you lose track of time. Aim for at least twenty items on your list. The first three to five will be

easy to identify. The next three to five may be more challenging, and the last ten will require even more thought. Keep going until you have listed twenty or more.

3. Next, flip to the next page of the notepad and write this: "Let's imagine that I was asked to choose just one item on this list, while others are to be discarded, and the one I chose will be fulfilled right now, which one will have the most impact on my life? Which will give me the greatest sense of achievement, happiness, and fulfilment?"

4. Flip back to the page where you have the list. Out of the items, which one jumps at you? Which one will answer the question above?

5. Write the answer below the question.

6. Next, cross out the item you have chosen from your list. Now you are left with nineteen or one less than the original number on your list.

7. Again, ask yourself the question you have asked before, "Let's imagine that I was asked to choose just one item on this list, while others are to be discarded, and the one I chose will be fulfilled right now, which one will have the most impact on my life? Which will give me the greatest sense of achievement, happiness, and fulfilment?". Again, put down your answer and cross out your chosen item from the list.

8. Repeat the process for the last time.

9. Now, you should have your three most important life work and goals in order of impact and importance.

These activities define your life goals and should be prioritised, requiring you to invest your time, resources, and energy. It's also important to mention that these tasks and goals will be refined and might get bigger as you embark on your journey. Often, we don't have the complete picture of what the Creator has in store for us, but stepping out in faith allows clarity to unfold daily. Just like when Abram was asked to leave his father's land for a place God promised to show him, he had no idea where he was going, but stepping out in faith brought him greater clarity. What you understand at the moment is just the tip of the iceberg of what you can achieve and do. Therefore, it would be inappropriate to say that all you have listed defines you entirely.

That is it about the simple steps to identifying what you were born to do.

Now that you have identified what you were born to do, what ignites your passion and purpose – the intersection of your gifts, values, and calling, and a manifestation of your unique contribution to the world, let's explore the kinds of work and how we can harness them for impact, fulfilment, and worthy compensation. This will be our focus in the next chapter.

Chapter Five

EXPLORING THE TWO DIMENSIONS OF WORK

Have you ever encountered the terms 'low-skilled' and 'high-skilled' labour? What immediately springs to mind when you hear these phrases? These terms give us a window into the two dimensions of work, which have existed since time immemorial and may be as old as the Earth itself.

Consider why one individual rises as early as 4 a.m. to clean the roads for minimal pay while another wakes up at the same hour but sits at their desk, engages in innovative thinking and brainstorming to solve problems, and earns multiple times more than the former. Both individuals were up early and engaged in tasks, yet one was compensated significantly more than the other. This stark contrast illustrates the different dimensions of work.

That's not all. Have you also considered why someone might work for four hours, for instance, and another person earns multiple times more in just thirty minutes than the individual who put in the four hours of hard work? This also emphasises that there are dimensions to work.

We've observed that work is what you are born to do; it's the task that aligns with your values, gifts, and purpose. As much as you are called to do something, it's essential to understand the dimensions of work. There are two main dimensions of work: handwork and brainwork. Handwork pertains to physical labour - tasks that require physical exertion or manual work, while brainwork relates to cognitive engagement -

involving creativity, innovation, and problem-solving abilities. Let's delve deeper into these dimensions.

ENGAGING YOUR CREATIVE ABILITY

It's interesting to note that the first dimension of work we were called to is inherent in our nature. For instance, it's the nature of a dog to bark and the nature of a bird to fly. They don't have to undergo formal training to do so; it comes naturally to them - they don't struggle with it. So, what is our inherent nature that defines the first dimension of work we were called to do? It's nothing but our creative ability. Let's delve into the creation narrative to explore this concept.

In the creation narrative, a divine board meeting among the Godhead was held to fashion a unique and extraordinary creation called man. Unlike previous creative endeavours, this assembly identified man's exceptional nature, which requires creativity and time to sculpt into an excellent product.

Remarkably, everything else on earth was created for this new product called man, which they were innovating about. The Earth, the sun, the moon, trees, flowers, fishes, and all other elements were designed with man in mind. Little wonder Apostle Paul exclaimed that God knew us before the earth's foundation; we existed before the Earth was created. This revelation is nothing short of inspiring. I didn't fully grasp what Paul meant until I understood the concept of the two creations. Everything that was created underwent the process of creation twice—whether it's the sun, the moon, chairs, cars, or any other entity. You can refer to the first chapter of this book for an explanation of the concept of the two creations.

When God created the light or animals, for instance, He simply declared, *'Let there be light,'*[27] and *'Let the earth produce living creatures according to their kinds,'*[28] and it was so. However, when it came to man, a unique process unfolded. Figuratively describing this process- when it came to the creation of man, God summoned the directors in charge, saying, *'Let us create man in our own image and likeness.'*[9] It's as if there is a corporation in heaven with a board of directors, and these directors had to convene for a meeting to create this new product- the earth had not seen anything like it before.

Before we continue, you need to come to terms with this: you are unique and special, and the earth had not seen anything like you before you were created. This realisation should ignite self-esteem as you embark on the journey to fulfil the reason for your existence and bring meaning to those around you. You possess gifts meant to enrich your world- you have got gifts for the world. Would you tug your head in pity or raise your shoulders in confidence and self-esteem as you achieve the greatness you were meant for?

The approach in creating man involved innovation and purposeful planning — defining what the product would look like and what it would accomplish. The result was the blueprint for the production process to create man. Afterwards, they worked on their plan, as we saw in the creation of the human spirit and the moulding of his body so that he could interact with the physical world. Little wonder Pierre Teilhard de Chardin said, *"We are not human beings having a spiritual experience. We are spiritual beings having a human experience."*

Yet, a crucial aspect demands attention. Since they decided what the product should be and what to do, they needed to provide the resources to achieve their purpose.

"What did they intend the product to be and do?" you may ask.

They said, *'Let us create man in our own image and likeness.'*[9] This means they wanted the new product to be like themselves. If there is anything we know about the Godhead up to the time of creating man, it is that they were creators. The opening statement of the Bible says, *'In the beginning, God created the heavens and the earth.'*[29] This shows that God is a creator. So, if the new product will take after their likeness, it must likewise be a creator. This reveals that man was created to be a creator, and any man who does not create lives below the standard and purpose of his existence. This is revealing! What do you think?

Now, take one to two minutes to ask yourself what was given to man to be like God as a creator.

What is your answer?

Are you able to come up with something?

Here is what He gave man to be a creator: the mind. God freely gave man the mind as a priceless gift for creating anything he desires. Although freely given, the mind plays a pivotal role in accomplishing the essence of man's existence. Unfortunately, this priceless gift is often undervalued and underutilised. Imagine a world where everyone puts their minds into creative mode to solve problems. Can you imagine how pleasant our world would be?

So it is evident that the very first dimension of work we were called to do is to engage our creative ability, which is brain or mental work. So before you embark on anything else as touching work, make sure you engage your innovative and creative ability. Creativity involves solving problems, and we can see that when the earth was in darkness and a terrible state, God came into the scene with his creative ability and brought beauty out of the earth's chaos. This is similar to what we were called to do. We are to bring beauty out of a terrible situation, motivation out of dejection, and solutions to problems.

When you engage your creative mind, you are being natural because that is our nature. Several things we call supernatural are supposed to be natural to us.

Mental work can be demanding, as energy is expended. In fact, it can be more demanding than

hand work, but it is more rewarding because it produces tangible benefits.

Before we leave this subject, it is essential to mention that every human has the ability to create - that is what makes us human. We were created to solve problems, to make our world better than we found it. We were deployed to the earth to establish the goodness of heaven on earth.

Some people may not know that they have something to offer the world. We all have gifts to give to the world. The story of a widow comes to mind. She was neck-deep in debt, and when her husband died, the creditors wanted to seize her children from her. She cried out to the prophet for help. I wouldn't know what she expected the prophet to do, probably to raise an offering for her to settle her debt or maybe pray so that the creditors would forget her debt. Many people seek assistance in this light; they want someone to give them money or help them pay their bills.

Instead of the prophet raising an offering for her or paying her debt, despite the faithfulness of her husband, who was likewise a prophet, he asked her, *"What shall I do for you? Tell me, what do you have in the house?"*[30] And she said, *"Your maidservant has nothing in the house but a jar of oil."*[30] **The solution to our problems is often with us. The challenge is that we have not recognised it.** She had the gift that could solve her financial problems, but she did not recognise it all along. She did not value what she had. The prophet told her what to do, and people paid her for the product she had from her gift. You are on the path of impact, fulfilment, and worthy compensation when you engage your creative ability, or in other words, when you do brain or mental work.

Take a few minutes to think about the following statements.[31]

1. Using a dull ax requires great strength, so sharpen the blade. That's the value of wisdom; it helps you succeed.

2. If the iron be blunt, and he do not whet the edge, then must he put to more strength: but wisdom is profitable to direct.

3. If the ax is dull, And one does not sharpen the edge, Then he must use more strength; But wisdom brings success.

4. If the axe is dull and he does not sharpen its edge, then he must exert more strength. Wisdom has the advantage of giving success.

5. If the axe is dull and he does not sharpen its edge, then he must exert more strength; but wisdom [to sharpen the axe] helps him succeed [with less effort].

6. Remember: The duller the ax the harder the work; Use your head: The more brains, the less muscle.

Is Handwork Without Significance?

In the context of our discussion, you might conclude that you do not need handwork if you can engage in mental work effectively. But is handwork without significance? Not at all. Handwork is equally vital for achieving the kind of results you want. Imagine coming up with a solution but never acting on it. **The solution would remain in the intangible world; only when you engage your thoughts with your hands will you get the desired results.** That's why I say, *"Never engage your hands until you have engaged your brain."* You need to engage both dimensions of work: your creative ability and your handwork, but let the work start by engaging your creative ability.

As we've seen earlier, God engaged His creative ability to envision what He wanted the earth to look like and the kind of man He wanted to be his steward. He didn't stop there; He also engaged His hands, moulding man from the earth—this is handwork. **Imagine having great ideas that were never implemented. Those ideas are worthless until they**

are implemented, and it takes handwork to implement them.

Another example is when Joseph gave Pharaoh the idea to prepare for the famine. If they hadn't engaged their hands to build storehouses, gather and store food, and implement other systems involved in the plan, they wouldn't have been able to overcome the famine so easily.

As Thomas Edison famously said, *"Genius is one per cent inspiration and ninety-nine per cent perspiration."* This view underscores the importance of generating ideas and working hard to bring them to fruition.

CREATE TIME FOR MENTAL WORK

Evidently, allocating more time to mental work enhances fulfilment and increases earnings. The ability to thoughtfully engage one's mind often leads to innovative solutions, creative breakthroughs, and heightened problem-solving skills. By intentionally dedicating time to mental work, individuals can tap into their creative potential and unlock new growth opportunities.

Consider the analogy of a sculptor carving a masterpiece from a block of marble. Just as the sculptor meticulously chisels away at the stone to reveal the beauty within, refine your thoughts and serve your ideas and gift to the world. Each stroke of insight contributes to creating something truly remarkable—a contribution to the world.

Creating time to engage your mind and creative ability is not a waste of time but saves you time. It's akin to sharpening the axe before using it on the tree. Don't be tempted to jump into a task without engaging your creative ability.

Be a creator. Shape your life. Mould your future.

ISRAEL DEMONSTRATING THE TWO DIMENSIONS OF WORK

The story of the people of Israel in Egypt is familiar, and it offers profound lessons, particularly regarding the dimensions of work we are considering. Arriving in Egypt during a famine, they found favour with Pharaoh, thanks to their brother, Joseph, Egypt's prime minister. Initially, they were welcomed and provided with land in Goshen, where they pursued their occupation as shepherds. However, with time and a change in leadership, their situation drastically shifted.

As a new Pharaoh came to power, unaware of or indifferent to Joseph's contributions, he grew fearful of the Israelites' growing numbers. Consequently, he subjected Israel to harsh treatment and forced them into slavery, tasked with labour-intensive projects and structures. This aspect of their experience exemplifies handwork, characterized by physical exertion and manual labour. The Israelites found themselves implementing innovations brought to them, rather than being involved in these projects conceptualization or planning stages. *"So the Egyptians made the Israelites their slaves. They appointed brutal slave drivers over them, hoping to wear them down with crushing labor. They forced them to build the cities of Pithom and Rameses as supply centers for the king."*[32].

They built cities for Pharaoh. The significance of this endeavour cannot be trivialised. Consider the magnitude of what a city represents. The specific structures they erected might not be clear. Given Egypt's status as a world power then, it's reasonable to assume that these structures were groundbreaking innovations, possibly contributing to Egypt's inclusion among the Seven Wonders of the Ancient World.

The Seven Wonders of the Ancient World are a testament to human creativity, representing unparalleled perfection and excellence. These wonders demonstrate both dimensions of work: brainwork and handwork. In Egypt, the people of Israel were primarily engaged in handwork, contributing manual labour to the construction projects. However, it's crucial to recognise that achieving such monumental feats requires more than physical effort alone. Engaging one's brain through innovation and problem-solving is essential. The synergy between mental and physical labour produces extraordinary results, captivating all who behold them, as seen with the impressive structures erected in Egypt.

The people of Israel spent many years in Egypt before their supernatural deliverance. During this time, they became accustomed to manual labour, relying heavily on their physical abilities rather than engaging their minds. Picture them repeatedly toiling away with their hands, devoid of access to the creative space where innovative ideas are conceived for years on end. Eventually, they forgot about their incredible creative potential. Would they remain enslaved for that long if they had engaged their minds? They had the number. Interestingly, the king and the taskmasters feared them because of their potential but never knew. *"And he said to his people, "Look, the people of the children of Israel are more and mightier than we; come, let us deal shrewdly with them, lest they multiply, and it happen, in the event of war, that they also join our enemies and fight against us, and so go up out of the land."*[33,34]

Their minds were imprisoned, and even after their physical deliverance, their mental liberation lagged behind. This was evident in their thought patterns throughout their journey to the promised land. Ironically, the land they were destined for did not require the handwork they had honed over the years. Instead, the cities were adorned with skyscrapers and structures beyond their imagination.

"I have given you a land for which you did not labour, and cities which you did not build, and you dwell in them; you eat of the vineyards and olive groves which you did not plant."[35]

"Attention, Israel! This very day you are crossing the Jordan to enter the land and oust nations that are much *bigger and stronger than you are. You're going to find huge cities with sky-high fortress-walls and gigantic people, descendants of the Anakites—you've heard all about them; you've heard the saying, "No one can stand up to an Anakite."*[36]

This time around, they needed to step into the boardroom. They had to harness their mental capacities to design systems to manage the structures rather than focusing solely on physical construction. They had to tap into their creative abilities even if they wanted to expand the existing structures. The generation that departed from Egypt was ill-prepared for this challenge. Consequently, God led them through the wilderness for forty years to raise a new generation that such mental constraints had not shackled.

We have come to the end of this chapter. It is time to flip to this book's next and last chapter.

Chapter Six

REST COMES AFTER WORK

We've come a long way in exploring the relationship between work and job. Before we delve into this new chapter, I want to take a moment to commend you for embarking on this enlightening journey through this book.

Now, let's focus on the concept of rest after work.

REAPING WHAT YOU HAVE SOWN: THE LAW OF HARVEST.

Interestingly, everyone desires success, but not everyone is willing to pay the price attached to it. As the saying goes, "You reap what you sow," emphasising the importance of planting before harvesting—a fundamental law of nature. If you seek a bountiful harvest, you must invest in preparing the soil, planting your seeds, and nurturing them as they grow to fruition. This, indeed, sounds like work. Engaging in work precedes realising your desired impact, fulfilment, and compensation.

The great teacher spoke of rest, highlighting two kinds during his teachings. The first type requires no effort to deserve or receive it; all one needs to do is accept it as a gift. His words exemplify this, *"Come to Me, all you who labour and are heavy laden, and I will give you rest."*[37] This can be likened to the peace of salvation, where the burden of sin and the torment of the devil are lifted. For instance, consider an individual entangled in drug addiction, spiralling toward a grim fate. If that person turns to the Lord Jesus, surrendering everything, they will find peace and solace in their soul. This compensation is unearned, emphasising that salvation is a gift bestowed by grace—undeserved favour freely given by the Creator. God's grace is defined as undeserved favour. Grace cannot be earned; it is freely given.

But it's worth noting that the great teacher didn't stop there; He continued, saying, *"Take My yoke upon you and learn from Me, for I am gentle and lowly in heart, and you will find rest for your souls. For My yoke is easy and My burden is light."*[38] This form of rest differs from the previous one that He mentioned. To attain this second form of rest, you have work to do. You must learn from Him and begin to think as He does. As you learn from Him, you'll start to emulate His actions. At the core of the great teacher's ministry was the pursuit of His life's purpose, as stated here: *"I must work the works of Him who sent Me while it is day; the night is coming when no one can work."*[39]

As seen above, it's evident that there is a time to work and another to refrain from work. On earth, there's a time for everything, and we should do what we're supposed to do when we're supposed to. Jesus was motivated to work when He had the time to do so, which should also be our motivation. Work during the daytime so you can rest when the night comes. This is, of course, figurative. It could mean that you should work in your prime years to rest when you're old or work while you're young so that you can rest when your physical strength is diminished. When you're old, you should have built systems to allow you to enjoy your retirement. It's important to note that rest comes after work, not vice versa. If you want to rest, do the work required to enjoy the kind of rest you desire. If you refuse to work when you're supposed to, you'll end up working when you're supposed to rest, or in other words, when you should be resting.

Do Your Work While You Are Young.

While at the university, I had the opportunity to address a group of young individuals. Interestingly, the message I conveyed to them still resonates with me, and I've encountered some who recounted the teaching. I shared a conviction close to my heart: the importance of engaging in our work while we're young. A verse from Jeremiah inspired this thought: *"It is good for a man to bear the yoke in his youth."*[40]

It is clear, as seen above that it is good to bear the yoke while you are young, but avoiding it is not. The 'yoke' here symbolises the work we are destined to undertake. As young individuals, we must seize the opportunities to fulfil our purpose. Failing to utilise the gifts bestowed upon us by the Creator may result in consequences suggestive of the parable of the servant who buried his talents and ended up punished.

What is a yoke? A yoke is a wooden beam typically used between a pair of oxen or other animals to enable them to pull together on a load. Metaphorically, 'bearing the yoke' refers to accepting a responsibility or following a particular path. Accepting responsibility can be equated to taking up the work you were wired to do on earth — gifting the world your talents, finding the intersection of your gifts, values, and calling, and manifesting your unique contribution to the world.

It is also noteworthy that bearing the yoke involves discipline. You cannot effectively pursue the work you were born to do without discipline. Embracing the yoke signifies a willingness to live a disciplined life, which is essential for success. Therefore, in other words, we could say, *'It is good to start living a disciplined life while you are young.'*

Do not forget that the great teacher also mentioned this, as we have seen before: *'**Take My yoke** upon you and learn from Me, for I am gentle and lowly in heart, and you will find rest for your souls.'* So, if you want to live an impactful and fulfilling life with worthy compensation, then live a disciplined life. Do not live without self-control.

Does it mean that you are only to bear the yoke in your youth alone? Or are you only to do your work in your youth alone? Not at all. As we have seen in this book, you do not retire from your work. You can retire from your job but not from your work. In fact, you are so full of resources and wonders that it will take a lifetime to express them all. As much as you do not retire from your work, it is good to start early. Do not wait until you are old before you start putting your energy into the essence of your creation. **Do not sacrifice your work on the altar of your job.**

If you start putting your energy into your work early, by the time you are old, you will have gone far with your work, and as you continue, you will see great returns on what you have invested over time.

Don't forget that rest comes after work. When God created the earth, He rested after He had worked. On the seventh day, He rested from His work. There is no justification for rest if one has not worked. *"And on the seventh day God ended His work which He had done, and*

He rested on the seventh day from all His work which He had done."[41] If you want to be a happy person as you age, then put in the work required when you have the time and strength. Remember that nothing is immune to change.

DON'T CONFUSE BEING BUSY WITH WORK.

In the hustle and bustle of modern life, it's easy to fall into the trap of equating busyness with productivity. We often find ourselves rushing from one task to another, constantly occupied with various activities, but are we genuinely getting meaningful work done? Being busy does not always translate to being productive or fulfilling our purpose.

There's a marked difference between being busy and being productive. Productive individuals accomplish meaningful tasks, while busy individuals simply get things done. We can judge whether you are productive or not by comparing your output to your input. Consequently, companies strive to maximize output while minimizing input, reducing costs and time required for production.

Translating this concept into personal productivity entails minimising the number of tasks needed to achieve a desired outcome. Busyness can sometimes lead to a sense of spinning the wheels without accomplishing anything significant. True work, on the other hand, is purposeful and intentional. It involves focusing our time and energy on tasks that align with our goals and values, moving us closer to our desired outcomes.

Imagine two individuals: one spends their days on various activities, always on the go but never achieving their long-term objectives, while the other allocates their time thoughtfully, prioritising tasks that contribute to their growth. The latter may appear less busy on the surface, but they are likely making more meaningful strides toward their goals.

Recognising that not all tasks are equally valuable or aligned with your goals is essential. Similarly, not all activities deserve your time and attention. One helpful framework for understanding this concept is the time management matrix, popularised by Stephen Covey in his book *"The 7 Habits of Highly Effective People."*

In this quadrant, tasks are categorised based on their urgency and importance, dividing them into four quadrants:

1. **Urgent and Important:** These tasks require immediate attention and directly contribute to your long-term goals and priorities. Examples include meeting deadlines, handling emergencies, and addressing critical issues.

2. **Important but Not Urgent:** Tasks in this quadrant are significant for your long-term success but may not require immediate action. They include activities like planning,

strategising, personal development, and relationship-building. You should spend most of your time here.

3. **Urgent but Not Important:** These tasks demand immediate attention but do not contribute significantly to your long-term goals and success. They are often distractions or interruptions that can consume time and energy if not appropriately managed. Examples include some emails, phone calls, and minor issues.

4. **Not Urgent and Not Important:** Tasks in this quadrant are neither urgent nor important and typically represent time-wasting activities or trivial matters. They include activities like excessive social media browsing, aimless web surfing, and other distractions.

Using the quadrant, you can evaluate tasks based on their positive impact and urgency, allowing you to prioritise effectively and focus on activities that align with your goals and values. This way, you can avoid getting caught up in a flurry of tasks and ensure your time is spent on what truly matters. If you want to learn more about this, pick up my book **"From Overwhelmed to Organised: A time management blueprint for busy professionals"**.

Find Your Work And Engage In It

As we conclude this book, I encourage you to discover the meaningful and impactful work you were meant to do. Invest your energy into pursuing it, and you will find rest, fulfilment, and rewards, both financial and many more. Don't just stay busy; instead, focus on finding the right work, as being busy does not always equate to achievement. Be intentional in your efforts and how you invest your time. Avoid wasting your energy on low-impact tasks.

UNLOCK YOUR POTENTIAL: DISCOVER THE TRANSFORMATIVE POWER OF MY OTHER BOOKS

Are you ready to take control of your life and achieve your dreams? Look no further. In addition to **"FIND YOUR WORK: Unlocking Your Path to Impact,**

Fulfilment, and Worthy Compensation," I have also written other books to help guide you on your journey to success.

In "**49 Words on Marble,**" I share wisdom and inspiration through powerful affirmations and motivational quotes for men and women, young and old. Positive mindset quotes to start your day and improve your life.

"**How to Live Above Circumstances**" teaches you how to be in control of your life and overcome any obstacle that may come your way. "**The Beatitudes**" explores the concept of living a life of happiness, prosperity, liberty, and blessedness.

In "**Write a Book Without Breaking a Sweat,**" I share the secrets to writing a book easily, making the process less daunting and more enjoyable. "**The Role of Graphic Design and Technology in Writing**" delves into the blogging world and how to develop a successful blog harnessing technology.

"From Overwhelmed to Organised: A Time Management Blueprint for Busy Professionals" reflects an insightful understanding of the challenges those leading demanding professional lives face. Drawing from personal experiences as a busy physician, author, coach, and digital solutions consultant, this book serves as a guide to take you from overwhelmed to organised.

"Leveraging The Power Of Seasons: Understanding and Taking Advantage of the Four Seasons of Life" isn't just a book; it's a roadmap to unlocking the treasures and opportunities within the ever-changing seasons of life. This masterpiece will guide you to take advantage of these seasons to achieve great success.

Each of these books offers unique insights and practical advice to help you navigate different aspects of your personal and professional life. Whether you're looking to cultivate a positive mindset, overcome challenges, manage your time effectively, or understand the different seasons of life, there's a book here to support you on your journey.

Take advantage of these transformative books. Check them out today by visiting my website [https://toyinobafemi.com.ng], Amazon kindle store [https://www.amazon.com/Toyin-H.-Obafemi/e/B081TLJKH7], or searching for them in your favourite bookstores.

THE AUTHOR

Dr Toyin Obafemi is an author, coach, and medical doctor, currently serving as a Senior Registrar in Internal Medicine with an interest in Dermatology.

With a commitment to helping people live better lives, Dr Obafemi has authored more than ten impactful books published and distributed globally. One of his books, **"From Overwhelmed to Organized: A Time Management Blueprint for Busy Professionals,"** reflects an insightful understanding of the challenges those leading demanding professional lives face. Drawing from personal experiences as a busy physician, author, coach, and digital solutions consultant, this book has earned recognition as an Amazon best-seller.

Having once experienced what it meant to be on an unfulfilling job, Dr Toyin Obafemi understands that the human spirit yearns for something more—something that brings joy and fulfilment. That's why he has written his latest book, **"FIND YOUR WORK: Unlocking Your Path to Impact, Fulfilment, and Worthy Compensation,"** to help readers discover the work they are wired to do, the kind that fills their souls with joy and fulfilment. This book is about finding fulfilment and earning worthy rewards—not just financial rewards but also the intangible rewards money can't buy.

Beyond his professional pursuits, Dr Obafemi finds fulfilment in his role as a dedicated spouse to Temitope and a loving father to two children, Oreofe and Inioluwa. This holistic approach to life underscores his value on personal relationships and balance amidst his numerous commitments.

****

Thank you for reading this book. I will love to hear from you. Kindly send your feedback to toyin@toyinobafemi.com.ng or leave me a review at your favourite bookstore. Thanks

****

REFERENCES

1. Must-Know Job Dissatisfaction Statistics [Current Data] • Gitnux [Internet]. [cited 2024 Apr 11]. Available from: https://gitnux.org/job-dissatisfaction-statistics/
2. Why 85% of People Hate their Jobs [Internet]. Staff Squared. 2019 [cited 2024 Apr 11]. Available from: http://staffsquared.com/blog/why-85-of-people-hate-their-jobs/
3. Essential Job Dissatisfaction Statistics In 2024 • ZipDo [Internet]. [cited 2024 Apr 11]. Available from: https://zipdo.co/statistics/job-dissatisfaction/
4. Genesis 3:17 Then to Adam He said, "Because you have heeded the voice of your wife, and have eaten from the tree of which I commanded you, saying, 'You shall not eat of it': "Cursed is the ground for your sake; In | New King James Version (NKJV) | Download The Bible App Now [Internet]. [cited 2024 Jun 15]. Available from: https://www.bible.com/bible/114/GEN.3.17.NKJV
5. Genesis 1:5 God called the light Day, and the darkness He called Night. So the evening and the morning were the first day. | New King James Version (NKJV) | Download The Bible App Now [Internet]. [cited 2024 Jun 15]. Available from: https://www.bible.com/bible/114/GEN.1.5.NKJV
6. Genesis 1:31 Then God saw everything that He had made, and indeed it was very good. So the evening and the morning were the sixth day. | New King James Version (NKJV) | Download The Bible App Now [Internet]. [cited 2024 Jun 15]. Available from: https://www.bible.com/bible/114/GEN.1.31.NKJV

7. Genesis 2:5 before any plant of the field was in the earth and before any herb of the field had grown. For the LORD God had not caused it to rain on the earth, and there was no man to till the ground | New King James Version (NKJV) | Download The Bible App Now [Internet]. [cited 2024 Jun 15]. Available from: https://www.bible.com/bible/114/GEN.2.5.NKJV
8. Genesis 2:15 Then the LORD God took the man and put him in the garden of Eden to tend and keep it. | New King James Version (NKJV) | Download The Bible App Now [Internet]. [cited 2024 Jun 15]. Available from: https://www.bible.com/bible/114/GEN.2.15.NKJV
9. Genesis 1:26 Then God said, "Let Us make man in Our image, according to Our likeness; let them have dominion over the fish of the sea, over the birds of the air, and over the cattle, over all the earth and over ev | New King James Version (NKJV) | Download The Bible App Now [Internet]. [cited 2024 Jun 15]. Available from: https://www.bible.com/bible/114/gen.1.26
10. Ephesians 1:4 just as He chose us in Him before the foundation of the world, that we should be holy and without blame before Him in love | New King James Version (NKJV) | Download The Bible App Now [Internet]. [cited 2024 Jun 15]. Available from: https://www.bible.com/bible/114/eph.1.4
11. Luke 9:62 But Jesus told him, "Anyone who puts a hand to the plow and then looks back is not fit for the Kingdom of God." | New Living Translation (NLT) | Download The Bible App Now [Internet]. [cited 2024 Jun 15]. Available from: https://www.bible.com/bible/116/LUK.9.62

12. Genesis 30:30 For what you had before I came was little, and it has increased to a great amount; the LORD has blessed you since my coming. And now, when shall I also provide for my own house?" | New King James Version (NKJV) | Download The Bible App Now [Internet]. [cited 2024 Jun 15]. Available from: https://www.bible.com/bible/114/GEN.30.30.NKJV
13. Matthew 7:16 You will know them by their fruits. Do men gather grapes from thornbushes or figs from thistles? | New King James Version (NKJV) | Download The Bible App Now [Internet]. [cited 2024 Jun 15]. Available from: https://www.bible.com/bible/114/MAT.7.16.NKJV
14. Matthew 6:20 Store your treasures in heaven, where moths and rust cannot destroy, and thieves do not break in and steal. | New Living Translation (NLT) | Download The Bible App Now [Internet]. [cited 2024 Jun 15]. Available from: https://www.bible.com/bible/116/MAT.6.20.NLT
15. John 9:23 Therefore his parents said, "He is of age; ask him." | New King James Version (NKJV) | Download The Bible App Now [Internet]. [cited 2024 Jun 15]. Available from: https://www.bible.com/bible/114/JHN.9.23.NKJV
16. Matthew 4:3 Now when the tempter came to Him, he said, "If You are the Son of God, command that these stones become bread." | New King James Version (NKJV) | Download The Bible App Now [Internet]. [cited 2024 Jun 15]. Available from: https://www.bible.com/bible/114/MAT.4.3.NKJV
17. Matthew 3:17 And suddenly a voice came from heaven, saying, "This is My beloved Son, in whom I am well pleased." | New King James Version (NKJV) |

Download The Bible App Now [Internet]. [cited 2024 Jun 15]. Available from: https://www.bible.com/bible/114/MAT.3.17.NKJV

18. Genesis 1:22 And God blessed them, saying, "Be fruitful and multiply, and fill the waters in the seas, and let birds multiply on the earth." | New King James Version (NKJV) | Download The Bible App Now [Internet]. [cited 2024 Jun 15]. Available from: https://www.bible.com/bible/114/GEN.1.22.NKJV

19. Genesis 1:28 Then God blessed them, and God said to them, "Be fruitful and multiply; fill the earth and subdue it; have dominion over the fish of the sea, over the birds of the air, and over every living thing tha | New King James Version (NKJV) | Download The Bible App Now [Internet]. [cited 2024 Jun 15]. Available from: https://www.bible.com/bible/114/GEN.1.28.NKJV

20. Proverbs 4:23 Keep your heart with all diligence, For out of it spring the issues of life. | New King James Version (NKJV) | Download The Bible App Now [Internet]. [cited 2023 Nov 11]. Available from: https://www.bible.com/bible/114/PRO.4.23.NKJV

21. Luke 19:13 So he called ten of his servants, delivered to them ten minas, and said to them, 'Do business till I come.' | New King James Version (NKJV) | Download The Bible App Now [Internet]. [cited 2024 Jun 15]. Available from: https://www.bible.com/bible/114/LUK.19.13.NKJV

22. Luke 19:13 So he called ten of his servants and gave them ten minas. 'Put this money to work,' he said, 'until I come back.' | New International Version (NIV) | Download The Bible App Now [Internet]. [cited 2024

Jun 15]. Available from: https://www.bible.com/bible/111/LUK.19.13

23. Luke 16:12 And if you have not been trustworthy with someone else's property, who will give you property of your own? | New International Version (NIV) | Download The Bible App Now [Internet]. [cited 2024 Jun 15]. Available from: https://www.bible.com/bible/111/LUK.16.12.NIV

24. Proverbs 18:16 A man's gift makes room for him, And brings him before great men. | New King James Version (NKJV) | Download The Bible App Now [Internet]. [cited 2024 Jun 15]. Available from: https://www.bible.com/bible/114/PRO.18.16.NKJV

25. Inam H. Leadership And The Boiling Frog Experiment [Internet]. Forbes. [cited 2024 Jun 15]. Available from: https://www.forbes.com/sites/hennainam/2013/08/28/leadership-and-the-boiling-frog-experiment/

26. Ecclesiastes 11:6 Sow your seed in the morning, and at evening let your hands not be idle, for you do not know which will succeed, whether this or that, or whether both will do equally well. | New International Version (NIV) | Download The Bible App Now [Internet]. [cited 2024 Jun 15]. Available from: https://www.bible.com/bible/111/ECC.11.6.NIV

27. Genesis 1:3 Then God said, "Let there be light"; and there was light. | New King James Version (NKJV) | Download The Bible App Now [Internet]. [cited 2024 Jun 15]. Available from: https://www.bible.com/bible/114/GEN.1.3.NKJV

28. Genesis 1:24 Then God said, "Let the earth bring forth the living creature according to its kind: cattle and creeping thing and beast of the earth, each according to its kind"; and it was so. | New King James Version

(NKJV) | Download The Bible App Now [Internet]. [cited 2024 Jun 15]. Available from: https://www.bible.com/bible/114/GEN.1.24.NKJV

29. Genesis 1:1 In the beginning God created the heavens and the earth. | New King James Version (NKJV) | Download The Bible App Now [Internet]. [cited 2024 Jun 15]. Available from: https://www.bible.com/bible/114/GEN.1.1.NKJV

30. II Kings 4:2 So Elisha said to her, "What shall I do for you? Tell me, what do you have in the house?" And she said, "Your maidservant has nothing in the house but a jar of oil." | New King James Version (NKJV) | Download The Bible App Now [Internet]. [cited 2024 Jun 15]. Available from: https://www.bible.com/bible/114/2KI.4.2.NKJV

31. Ecclesiastes 10:10 - Wisdom and Folly [Internet]. Bible Hub. [cited 2024 Jun 15]. Available from: https://biblehub.com/ecclesiastes/10-10.htm

32. Exodus 1:11 So the Egyptians made the Israelites their slaves. They appointed brutal slave drivers over them, hoping to wear them down with crushing labor. They forced them to build the cities of Pithom and Rames | New Living Translation (NLT) | Download The Bible App Now [Internet]. [cited 2024 Jun 15]. Available from: https://www.bible.com/bible/116/EXO.1.11.NLT

33. Exodus 1:9 And he said to his people, "Look, the people of the children of Israel are more and mightier than we | New King James Version (NKJV) | Download The Bible App Now [Internet]. [cited 2024 Jun 15]. Available from: https://www.bible.com/bible/114/EXO.1.9.NKJV

34. Exodus 1:10 come, let us deal shrewdly with them, lest they multiply, and it happen, in the event of war, that

they also join our enemies and fight against us, and so go up out of the land." | New King James Version (NKJV) | Download The Bible App Now [Internet]. [cited 2024 Jun 15]. Available from: https://www.bible.com/bible/114/EXO.1.10.NKJV

35. Joshua 24:13 I have given you a land for which you did not labor, and cities which you did not build, and you dwell in them; you eat of the vineyards and olive groves which you did not plant.' | New King James Version (NKJV) | Download The Bible App Now [Internet]. [cited 2024 Jun 15]. Available from: https://www.bible.com/bible/114/JOS.24.13.NKJV

36. Deuteronomy 9 | MSG Bible | YouVersion [Internet]. [cited 2024 Jun 15]. Available from: https://www.bible.com/bible/97/DEU.9.MSG

37. Matthew 11:28 Come to Me, all you who labor and are heavy laden, and I will give you rest. | New King James Version (NKJV) | Download The Bible App Now [Internet]. [cited 2024 Jun 15]. Available from: https://www.bible.com/bible/114/MAT.11.28.NKJV

38. Matthew 11:29 Take My yoke upon you and learn from Me, for I am gentle and lowly in heart, and you will find rest for your souls. | New King James Version (NKJV) | Download The Bible App Now [Internet]. [cited 2024 Jun 15]. Available from: https://www.bible.com/bible/114/MAT.11.29.NKJV

39. John 9:4 I must work the works of Him who sent Me while it is day; the night is coming when no one can work. | New King James Version (NKJV) | Download The Bible App Now [Internet]. [cited 2024 Jun 15]. Available from: https://www.bible.com/bible/114/JHN.9.4.NKJV

40. Lamentations 3:27 It is good for a man to bear The yoke in his youth. | New King James Version (NKJV) | Download The Bible App Now [Internet]. [cited 2024 Jun 15]. Available from: https://www.bible.com/bible/114/LAM.3.27.NKJV
41. Genesis 2:2 And on the seventh day God ended His work which He had done, and He rested on the seventh day from all His work which He had done. | New King James Version (NKJV) | Download The Bible App Now [Internet]. [cited 2024 Jun 15]. Available from: https://www.bible.com/bible/114/GEN.2.2.NKJV

www.ingramcontent.com/pod-product-compliance
Lightning Source LLC
Chambersburg PA
CBHW031418210526
45464CB00005B/1937